HILL 112

Battles of the Odon

Battleground Europe

HILL 112
Battles of the Odon

Tim Saunders

LEO COOPER

This book is dedicated in gratitude
to the late J.D. Spinney Esq
History master and source of inspiration,
Clayesmore School, Dorset.

Other books in the series by Tim Saunders
Gold Beach-JIG – Normandy
Hell's Highway – Market Garden
Nijmegen – Market Garden
The Island – Market Garden

First published 2001, Reprinted 2002
by
LEO COOPER
an imprint of
Pen & Sword Books Limited
47 Church Street, Barnsley, South Yorkshire S70 2AS
Copyright © Tim Saunders 2001, 2002

ISBN 0 85052 737 6

A CIP record of this book is available
from the British Library

Printed in the United Kingdom by
CPI UK

For up-to-date information on other titles produced under the Leo Cooper
imprint, please telephone or write to:
Pen & Sword Books Ltd, FREEPOST SF5, 47 Church Street
Barnsley, South Yorkshire S70 2BR
Telephone 01226 734222

CONTENTS

ACKNOWLEDGEMENTS

Firstly, I would like to thank veterans of the battle, particularly members of 43rd Wessex Association, for so freely giving their time to talk to me about their experiences on Hill 112. In some cases, they relived some horrific moments, in order that what actually happened on that hillside is put on the record. Secondly, as with all other authors in the Battleground Europe series, this author is indebted to the present day regimental headquarters of the many British units that fought at Hill 112. The staff responsible for archives, be they overworked regimental secretaries or very knowledgeable volunteers, all generously and promptly answered a multitude of enquiries on my behalf. The archives of the Tank Museum, at Bovington, Dorset and Peter Beal were particularly useful in ensuring that the part played by the armour in the battle has been properly reflected. However, I would particularly like to thank the staff of that wonderful resource for the military historian, the Prince Consort's Library in Aldershot, who were, as ever, outstanding. I am most grateful for the loan of diaries and photographs from various other sources.

Any military history of the Second World War that seeks to portray an action through both sides' eyes must examine sources in languages other than English. As an author who is unable to speak either German or French competently, I am greatly indebted to Anne Fox, who gave her time generously to translate many pages of documents.

Finally, in common with most authors, I have to sincerely thank my family for their forbearance and encouragement to complete this project. They also bore the brunt of reading and checking the all too numerous drafts of this book. However, as always, responsibility for errors is entirely mine.

INTRODUCTION

Squeezed between the two better known operations of EPSOM and GOODWOOD, the fighting at Hill 112, the battle called Operation JUPITER, is less well known but deserves wider understanding and appreciation. During July 1944, readers of British or German newspapers would seldom fail to find a reference to, or story about, Hill 112, and within the two armies, newsletters extensively featured reports on the fighting. This book aims to share what was at the time common knowledge of the battles fought at Hill 112 with the modern reader.

As this book is a guide, I have avoided controversy and excessive commentary, preferring to let powerful events speak for themselves. However, following repeated questions from those who have seen Spielberg's film *Saving Private Ryan* and reflecting on the comments that it contains on the British part of the Normandy Campaign, I have included a section on Montgomery's strategy. Concerning the quality of the British Second Army in battle, I let action speak for itself. I have also taken care to cover the part played by the supporting arms, such as the gunners of the anti-tank regiments Royal Artillery whose, highly significant role is frequently overlooked in accounts of battles.

Our ground for this guide lies between the rivers Odon and Orne. The River Odon is a small stream in a narrow, steep-sided, valley that lies to the north of the area and has few crossing points. The Odon valley was an obstacle to movement. The banks, hedges and the steep sided tree-lined stream made life difficult for both tracked and wheeled vehicles. During the month that the frontline rested on Hill 112, the valley became justifiably known as 'Death Valley'.

Rising from the close confines of the valley are the open slopes of the central part of our area: Hill 112. The feature can be seen on the skyline from much of the western portion of the Allied lodgement area but, with its gentle slopes, it can hardly be described as dominating. However, when standing on the crest, the fields of fire and, more importantly, observation are impressive. A senior German officer, no doubt returning from a recce of the area, was overheard by a Resistance informer to say 'He who holds Hill 112, holds Normandy'. Even today, with much post-war building along the Caen to Bayeux road, it is easy to understand the importance attached to Hill 112 by both sides and why so much blood was spent contesting its possession. Looking closer, the slopes of the hill have a far from uniform profile. In some directions the slopes are concave and in others convex, which, as we shall see, both the attacking and defending infantry found to be highly significant.

The small Norman farming communities of the area lie mainly in the low ground. The buildings were strongly built from the warm honey-coloured limestone of the region and, despite suffering much destruction and the presence of modern in-fill housing, retain much of their character.

Forming the eastern and southern boundary of our area is the River Orne. It is larger than the Odon and meanders through a broad valley, with flanks that sweep down from the open ridges and broad plateau of Hill 112. Beyond lie the temptingly open plains of Northern France, ideal for a speedy armoured advance eastwards to Germany.

Those few square miles were to be the scene of some of the hardest and most protracted fighting during the Normandy Campaign. Indeed, one brigade commander who had experienced the 'trenchlock' of the Western Front, said of the battle, 'In these conditions, comparable only in my experience, to the bombardment at Passchendaele, the Division was to remain in action for fourteen days'.

This guide will put the battle for Hill 112 into the context of Montgomery's campaign strategy, and introduce the formations and units of both sides. But, above all, we will hear from the men who fought so tenaciously at Hill 112.

ADVICE FOR VISITORS

Preparation and planning are important prerequisites for an enjoyable and successful tour of any battlefield. This section gives some useful advice to those who are travelling to Normandy for the first time and acts as a checklist for the more seasoned traveller. Remember, some Second World War wisdom 'Time spent in reconnaisance is seldom wasted' or the more soldierly and memorable 'Prior planning and preparation prevents poor performance'.

Travel to Normandy

Most visitors travelling to the Normandy battlefields do so by car. However, with the area's proximity to ports, an increasing number of hardy souls are cycling around the battlefields. Whichever method one chooses to travel around Normandy, anyone whose journey originates in the UK has to get across or under the Channel. A wide range of crossing options are available. The nearest ferry service to Hill 112 is the Brittany Ferries route which delivers the visitor from Portsmouth to Ouistreham, less than twenty minutes drive from Caen alongside Sword Beach. This crossing is slightly longer than others; six hours during the day or six hours thirty minutes overnight. Further away, one hour thirty minutes drive to the west, is the port of Cherbourg, which is served by sailings from Portsmouth, Southampton and Poole (four hours thirty minutes to five hours). Equidistant from Hill 112 but to the east is le Havre, which is served by ferries that leave the UK from Portsmouth and Southampton. Choice for most visitors depends on the convenience of the sailing times and, of course, relative costs. Do not forget special offers. To the east of Normandy are the shorter, and consequently cheaper, crossings in the Boulogne and Calais area. For those who dislike ferries there is the Channel Tunnel, but this option, though quicker, is usually more expensive. From the Calais area, Hill 112 can be easily reached via the new autoroutes in under four hours but bear in mind tolls cost up to £15. This can be reduced to about £10 by avoiding the new Pont de Normandie. It is worth checking out all the options available and make your selection of route based on UK travel, ferry times and, of course cost. French law requires you to carry a full driving licence and a vehicle registration document. Do not forget your passport and a GB sticker if you do not have EU number plates with the blue national identifier square.

Insurance

It is important to check that you are properly insured to travel to France. Firstly, check with your insurance broker to ensure that your car is properly covered for driving outside the UK and, secondly, make sure you have health cover. Form E111, available from main post offices, grants the bearer reciprocal treatment rights in France but, even so, the visitor may wish to consider a comprehensive package of travel insurance. Such packages are available from a broker or travel agent. It is a legal requirement for a driver to carry a valid certificate of motor insurance. Be warned that without insurance, repatriating the sick or injured is very expensive, as is return of vehicles.

Accommodation

There are plenty of options ranging from hotels in Caen to very well-run campsites, with all other grades of accommodation in between. In the centre of Caen, near the Bassin St Pierre are the three-star *Ibis* and *Mercure* hotels (tel: (0)2 31 47 24 24), which are near to a wide variety of local restaurants. Slightly further from the centre (and cheaper) is *Hotel de France* (tel: (02) 31 52 16 99), which is popular with touring parties. Further contacts are available from the French Tourist Office, 178 Picadilly, London, W1V 0AL (0891 244 123). Further details of accommodation and travel amenities are available from the office of Calvados Tourisme, Place du Canada, 14000 Caen, France. To telephone from the UK dial 00 33, drop the 0 necessary for ringing within France and dial 2 31 86 53 30.

Maps

Good maps are an essential prerequisite to a successful battlefield visit. Best of all is a combination of contemporary and modern maps. The *Battleground Series* of course, provides a variety of maps. However, a full map sheet enables the visitor or indeed those who are exploring the battlefield from the comfort of their armchair, to put the battle in a wider context. A contemporary 1:25,000 map sheet, overprinted by 43rd Wessex Division's G Int branch on 8 July 1944, is available from the Keep Military Museum, Bridport Road, Dorchester, Dorset, DT1

The River Odon running high, fast and deep with winter rain.

Close country of the Odon valley; hedges and ditches ensured short fields of fire.

1RN for £4.99 including postage and packing. It shows the woods and roads as they were before the intervention of modern agriculture. Overprinted are the German positions that had been located by patrols and air reconnaissance prior to the battle. A number of modern map series are available in both the UK and Normandy. Most readily available in both countries are the Michelin 1:200,000 Yellow Series. Sheet 54 covers the British and US D-Day, build-up and break-out battle areas and is useful for getting around the Normandy battlefields and its ports. Better still are the *Institut Geographique National (IGN)* 1:100,000 *Serie Vert* (Green Series) maps. Sheet 6, *Caen-Cherbourg-Normandie*, covers most of the Normandy battle area. Normally only available in the UK at a specialist map shop, they can, however, be procured as a special order through high street book shops such as *Waterstones*. The *Serie Verte* maps have the advantage of showing contours and other details such as unmade roads and tracks. Sheet 6 is a good compromise if you are visiting several sites and wish to use a single map. The most detailed maps, readily available in France, are the *IGN Serie Bleue* in 1:25,000 scale. The Hill 112 area is covered on two sheets: 15 12 E Caen, which includes Eterville and the Northern part of Hill 112, and sheet 15 13 E, which covers the southern part of the Operation JUPITER area. The best supplier of maps in Caen is *Hemispheres*, a small but comprehensively supplied retailer, located in *Rue Croisiers*. Directions are easily obtainable from the information office opposite the Cathedral. However, if you are planning your tour well in advance, large retailers in the UK can order the *Serie Bleue* maps, given sufficient notice. When purchasing maps, do try to find ones that show the southern portion of the *Périphérique*, which was completed in the late nineties. The recent roadworks have greatly changed access to the Hill 112 battlefield and it is advisable to have an up-to-date map.

Courtesy

The Hill 112 area is open farmland. However, many of the surrounding villages were also a part of the battlefield and, consequently, were heavily fought over. Please respect private property in both open country and villages, particularly avoiding driving on unmade up farm tracks and entering non-public areas in villages. Adequate views of the scene of the action can be enjoyed from public land. In all cases, please be

The open plateau of Hill 112. The battlefield today is bisected by electricity pylons.

careful not to block roads by careless car parking. The people of Normandy extend a genuine welcome to those who come to honour the memory of their Allied liberators. To preserve this welcome please be courteous to the local people.

Warning: Unexploded Ordnance

Most of the Normandy battlefields were fought over for a matter of hours or a few days at the most. However, at Hill 112, the front fluctuated a little but remained bisecting the feature for over a month. Despite the improvements in the manufacture of shells by 1944, there are still a significant number of unexploded items of both British and German ordnance in the ground. These are potentially dangerous and are regularly turned up by the plough. It is worth bearing in mind that these items are twenty-five years younger than those found on First World War battlefields and, consequently, the explosive filling will have decayed to a lesser degree. It is best not to touch anything metallic found on the battlefield.

Enjoy the tour.

Hill 112 in 1944 shortly after the war had moved on.

CHAPTER ONE

OPERATION EPSOM
Taurus over the Odon

Most of the area covered by Operation EPSOM is not within the geographical scope of this book. However, the 'high water mark' of the offensive reached Hill 112. This chapter gives sufficient background to allow the visitor to Hill 112 to understand the context of the battle and describes, in greater detail, 11th Armoured Division's capture and defence of the feature during the latter stages of EPSOM.

Operation EPSOM was Montgomery's third attempt to take Caen, which had been the 3rd Division's D-Day objective some twenty days earlier. On this occasion his aim was to envelop the city from the west and to threaten to break out onto the more open ground south of the city. This would have secured the city's important road and rail junctions and put the Allies onto the shortest route to Berlin. The Germans were bound to react to this attack and, in anticipation, they had been forced to keep the bulk of their panzer divisions facing the British Second Army. With the German armour effectively tied down around Caen the Americans could expand the Allied lodgement and subsequently breakout in the west more easily. Following a preliminary attack by 49th West Riding Division on Rauray, Lieutenant General O'Connor's VIII Corps was to advance rapidly on a narrow front with 15th Scottish Division, to the River Odon. The seizure of the Odon

Bernard Law Montgomery

15

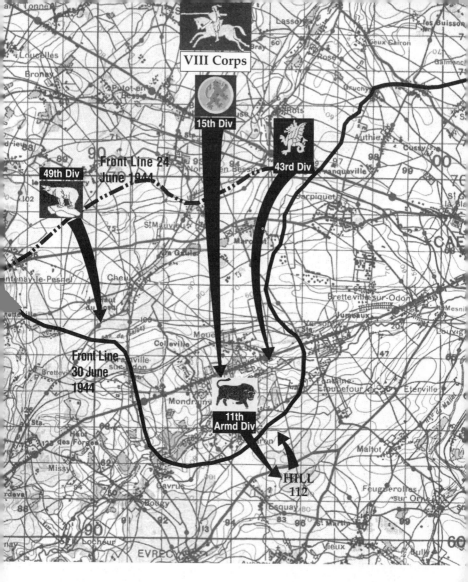

bridges was to be the cue for 11th Armoured Division to dash for the River Orne crossings and the open tank country beyond.

Beginning on 25 June 1944, EPSOM was slow going for both the 49th West Riding and 15th Scottish Divisions. The salient or 'Scottish Corridor' that they created, was too narrow and with too many troops fighting off a single road. Consequently, VIII Corps was unable to develop momentum against the 'loathsome' but determined soldiers of 12th *Hitler Jugend* SS

Panzer Division. To make matters worse, 49th Division's advance onto the Rauray spur was checked by the young SS soldiers, making the already exposed 'Scottish Corridor' even more vulnerable to counter attack. The British armoured regiments suffered heavy tank losses, as they advanced into the depth of the Hitler Youth positions. On foot, the infantry's casualties mounted under a relentless fire from well-concealed *Spandaus* and from the dreaded *Nebelwerfers*. The advance effectively became bogged down on the Caen – Villers Bocage road.

Two teenage SS panzer grenadiers belonging to the 12th SS *Hitler Jugend* Panzer Division.

A contemporary artist's impression of the seizure of the Tourmauville Bridge. The width of the River Odon is exaggerated.

On 27 June 1944, at 1800 hours, 2/Argyle and Sutherland Highlanders of 227 Brigade seized the small but vital Tourmauville bridge over the River Odon. Amid the fog of war they had abandoned direct attacks and succeeded in slipping through a gap in the *Hitler Jugend's ad hoc* defences by commendable guile. Reaching the narrow stone bridge at the bottom of the narrow, steep sided Odon Valley they dug in and held on until reinforced. The tenuous toehold of 15th Scottish Division's principal objective, boldly but belatedly, completed EPSOM's first phase.

11th Armoured Division advances to Hill 112

Half an hour after the Argyles reached the Tourmauville Bridge, the leading Shermans of C Squadron, 23/Hussars, led by Lieutenant Pratt, 'with great dash' reached the bridge, much

The Tourmauville Bridge taken by men of the 2/Argyle and Sutherland Highlanders, 27 June 1944.

to the relief of the Scots. Crossing the bridge, as described in their regimental history, the tanks:

'... *ground along in low gear up a steep and twisting track through wooded and difficult country until they came out just south of the village of Tourmauville [south of the Odon], where, for the first time, they were able to fan out on ground that gave a good field of fire. Commanders and gunners strained their dust filled eyes. Were some of those bushes camouflaged tanks? One German experienced what was probably the greatest shock of his life. He appeared in a small civilian car from the direction of Esquay. Lance Corporal Evans put an armour piercing shot through the car at a range of twenty yards. Surprisingly the driver managed to get out and, though pursued by Corporal Hoggins with a Sten gun, he got away and was last seen going very fast in the direction of Esquay. This was followed almost at once by a short engagement with some guns and infantry in the area of Garvus.'*

Shermans of the 23rd Hussars heading towards the River Odon with a Honey light tank in the vanguard.

Caen to Tourville road and the start line for 139 Brigade's advance to the River Odon to establish a bridgehead.

By 19.00 hours, both of the depleted B and C Squadrons were across the bridge, supported by Major Mackenzie's H Company, 8/Rifle Brigade (8/RB) who, in their half-tracks, had accompanied the tanks.

Following up, and trying to fight their way through the traffic jam of 15th Scottish Division's supply convoys and

Men of the 6th Royal Scots Fusiliers advance under cover of a smoke screen at the outset of Operation Epsom.

knocked out vehicles, were 11th Armoured Division's infantry brigade. At 20.00 hours, accurate information was scarce. Had we taken the bridge? Where were the enemy? No one knew anything for sure, except that 159 Brigade was to cross the Odon by dark. The commander of 159 Brigade gave what his battalion commanders considered an unreasonable H hour for the advance, but the force of his personality prevailed. After one of those confrontations, unique to battle, the tired, concerned and fearful commanding officers were ordered to be in position by 21.30 hours! 'An order is an order! Carry it out or take the consequences! Into battle!'

In the gathering darkness, after a chaotic advance, the leading battalions, 1/Herefords on the right and the 4/King's Shropshire Light Infantry (KSLI) on the left, both managed to cross the Odon. 3/Monmouths (Mons) occupied defences on the north bank as brigade reserve. Major Ned Thornburn's description of 4/KSLI's advance to the Odon graphically portrays the type of problems the brigade encountered:

'We set out along this forest avenue at full light infantry pace, interspersed with stretches at the double. I ran from one platoon commander to the next explaining what the plan for the attack was. Mine was the second or third company in the order of march, so at least I didn't have the responsibility of trying to achieve the impossible task of reaching the main [Caen - Villers Bocage] road. I think we assumed that the enemy would be too alarmed by our numbers to show themselves (how naïve one can

Site of the ornamental bridge across the Odon. This rickety girder bridge is positioned on the original abutments.

be!). By 21.15 I knew we had missed the artillery barrage... I got my two leading platoons lying down along the edge of the forest... I gave the word to commence the attack and we crossed the road. 'Time spent in reconnaissance is never wasted', the book says, but of course no one had done any reconnaissance on this start line and when we attempted to charge forward we found the thickest thorn hedge any of us had ever seen in our lives – utterly and completely unappeasable. I ran along the road for 100 yards or so until I found a gate, and we all walked through it very politely! Little did I think that D Company would deliver its first attack in single file with the company commander leading and reading his map! ...we walked safely straight down to the river where, believe it or not we found straight in front of us an ornamental bridge ...and we walked 400 yards up a steepish pathway to find ourselves at the gates of the Chateau de Baron. We were on our objective without a single casualty and there was not a soul to be seen anywhere. It was about 22.45.'

The remainder of the Battalion followed on twenty minutes later.

The Herefords had a less torrid time by simply following the road down to the Tourmauville Bridge and deploying beyond the Argyles. By dawn the bridgehead was firmly held by the dug-in 159 Brigade, supported by tanks of 29 Armoured Brigade. An excellent platform for exploitation had been formed, from which 11th Armoured Division's tanks could advance to the Orne.

After a sleepless night, at dawn on 28 June 1944, two enemy Mark IVs were spotted on Hill 112 and engaged at long range resulting in 'one tank being knocked out and one being damaged'. These two tanks were a part of 5 Company, 12 SS Panzer Regiment who were leaguered up in Esquay, with their exhausted crews grabbing what rest they could. Otherwise, it was relatively quiet as 4/KSLI's history describes:

A *Panzerkampfwagen* Mk IV moves up to counter the advance of VIII Corps in the area of Hill 112.

'Although no attack came in, a number of the enemy infiltrated between the company positions and made a nuisance of themselves. They first crept up and attacked the RAP at a range of about thirty yards, wounding two stretcher bearers. The reaction of the battalion was fierce, resulting in the expenditure of large quantities of ammunition with little to show for it. These were early days and the battalion was still green. It was soon realized, however, that indiscriminate fire against stray Germans in close country was of little value, and later these men – they were called snipers although they were very ordinary German infantry [Hitler Jugend] with the most rudimentary ideas of musketry – were hunted by small parties of men with more success, about ten of them being killed or captured.'

Meanwhile, the commanding officer of the 23/Hussars, taking advantage of the Germans' relative quiescence, dispatched B Squadron to the top of Hill 112. However, a *Luftwaffe* motorized flak battery, I/53, had deployed onto Hill 112, with its 88mm guns in the ground role.

Luftwaffe personnel man an 88mm gun in the anti-tank role in the vicinity of Hill 112.

11th Armd Div

Luftwaffe 88mm and elements of 12 SS Pz Div supported by 8 Nebelwerfer Bde

Hill 112

Bas de Mouen

Min de Cheux

Miebord

Quarriers

Tourville

Gournay

68

...mauville

11

Baron

Vilains

C...x des Filandriers

le Bon Repas

Esquay

Bas d'Esquay

83

R 484 63

113

0   1000   2000   3000

YARDS

Chateau de Baron. It was used as Battalion HQ and Regimental Aid Post by the 4th King's Shropshire Light Infantry during Epsom.

'C Squadron remained where they were to give B Squadron covering fire as they moved forward. Skirting the ruins of Baron, B Squadron approached the hill from the north as the lie of the ground gave most cover for an approach from that direction and most of the enemy fire seemed to be coming from the south [western] slope of the hill. They went for some time over open, undulating country, which was good going for tanks, reminiscent of the Yorkshire Wolds. One tank was hit by a 50 millimetre shot which broke its track, and Lieutenant. Cochrane's tank was hit and destroyed. The crew got out and came under heavy fire from both sides ...The Squadron had meanwhile, by moving round a little further to the east, had established itself on the northern part of the hill. The enemy opposition in the area consisted of dug-in tanks and infantry in position in a small wood. Their tanks had alternative sites to move to under cover and were almost impossible to get at. An attempt was made to knock them out with some self-propelled anti-tank guns which were under our command and were sent forward with B Squadron. It was unsuccessful. Medium artillery was tried without effect. Finally, rocket firing Typhoons were called up but the Tigers [almost certainly Mark IVs and Panthers of 12th SS Panzer Regiment] *were well camouflaged and the pilots were unable to locate them. The Gunners put down red smoke to indicate the target. One round fell amongst*

our own tanks and the hillside was immediately covered in
yellow smoke, tins of which were issued to each tank so that it
could signal to our aircraft and assure them that it was friendly.
It often worked. On this occasion the CO dropped the smoke in
the turret of his tank to the great amusement of those who were
near enough to see what happened and the discomfiture of his
crew who found it rather overpowering.'

B Squadron was joined by C Squadron, H Company 8/RB and Regimental Headquarters. Despite much manoeuvring and firing they could not shift the German anti-tank guns and losses of Shermans mounted. The smoke from burning tanks, including the commanding officer's, started to billow across the battlefield. As the 23/Hussar's ammunition was running low, H Company were sent forward to take the orchard on the top of the hill, which they did with some casualties. Rifleman Roland Jefferson recalls,

'Hill 112 will always be remembered as our initiation into the
real hatefulness of war. We found ourselves in a cornfield on the
[western] *flanks overlooking the valley leading to Esquay.'*

It would appear that the enemy were a largely armoured force, with only a company of panzer grenadiers on the hilltop, who fell back as the British infantry closed in on them.

The news of the British capture of Hill 112 was passed to 8 *Werfer* Brigade by field telephone. *Feldwebel* Doorn, who answered the phone ran to get 6 Battery's commander, who received the following message:

'Sir, the British are on top of the hill. A Sherman tank has
stopped just five metres from one of our observation posts. For
God's sake don't ring – they'll hear it. We'll try and get back
somehow. I don't know what has happened to Leutnant Wernike
and Leutnant Nitschmann. I think they must have been
overrun.'

In order to confirm what had happened, *Feldwebel* Doorn was dispatched with a patrol up the open southern slopes of the hill and was quickly seen and driven off with two casualties. His report to *Hauptmann* Gengl confirmed their worst fears:

'It's not just a couple of tanks up there! Tommy's got anti-
tank guns and part of a machine gun unit.'

12th SS Panzer Regiment hastily planned counter-attacks. Panthers of 1/Battalion attacked from the south and Mark IVs of 2/Battalion came from the south-west. SS-*Scharfuhrer* Willy

23rd Hussars' Shermans and M3 half-track of the 8/Rifle Brigade at the foot of Hill 112.

Kretschmar, aged twenty, commanded one of the tanks climbing the slope from Esquay.

> 'When I came to the end of the cover provided by the little wood, I halted and had a good look around. With my binoculars I searched the country stretching away to our left, looking for tanks and anti-tank guns. Nothing suspicious! 'Panzer advance!' I shouted. We had advanced ten or fifteen metres when there was a sudden crash. The sparks flew. We had been hit from the right. 'Reverse' I shouted. SS-Mann Schneider reacted like lightning. Back we shot at full speed. Back into cover of the wood. And only just in time! The Engländer almost got us! A hairs-breadth in front of our panzer, armour-piercing solid shot was tearing horrible black furrows in the green grass.'

The counter-attack of the *Hitler Jugend* was beaten off but not before knocking out more Shermans, some of which were battle casualty replacements and had just arrived. Further advance by 23/Hussars from the narrow salient, however, proved to be impossible. Despite their failure to retake Hill 112, the ring of panzers and the *Luftwaffe*'s 88mm guns, to the south of the feature, contained the spearhead of 29 Armoured Brigade. I SS Panzer Corps was not, however, content with containing the British, they wanted Hill 112 back! The young soldiers of 12th SS Panzer Regiment were to counter-attack again. SS-

Obersturmführer Kaendler of 5 Company was with them:

'My gunner, Willi Schnittfinke, reported a defect in the electric firing mechanism. We had to halt, and after a quick repair we were some distance behind the three panzers manoeuvring in front of us. SS-Sturmbannführer Mueller was also hanging back behind Porsch and Kunze. Kunze, in the

Men of the *Hitler Jugend* Division manning a PAK 75 at Hill 112.

A German Mk V (Panther) burns after a direct hit.

leading panzer, referring no doubt to those hanging back, shouted over the wireless: "It's all the bloody same to me! Advance!" Two hundred yards from the little wood Kunze's panzer was knocked out. Only the gunner and driver baled out. Groeter, the driver, was visibly shaken. He said the shell had gone clean between his legs.'

The counter-attack failed.

German six-barrelled mortar, *Nebelwerfer*, or 'Moaning Minnie'.

After almost twelve hours in action on the exposed hillside, 23/Hussars could not be replenished with ammunition in broad daylight, so they were relieved by 3/RTR at about 15.00 hours. 23/Hussars had lost thirty-three troopers killed in action, thirty-three wounded and six missing. G Company 8/RB joined 3/RTR on Hill 112. Rifleman Norman Habertin recalls shortly after their arrival on the hill-top:

'The storm broke. The enemy had been watching us settle down and before a single trench had been dug, down came those dreaded "moaning minnies". There was nothing to do but lie down and bite the earth. A half-track a few yards away went up in flames and when the mortaring finally stopped, the complete battalion was in a state of utter chaos. All the company vehicles were mixed up, no one knew where their section or platoon was, wounded men were yelling for help and nobody in authority could get any orders carried out.'

8/RB were not the only occupants of the Hill. It was not long before the infantry discovered that some of the enemy bunkers were still occupied.

'Suddenly a scraggy-looking beggar in field grey appeared from a hedge with his hands in the air. He was rushed off at the point of a bayonet. He kept looking back, frightened or perhaps worried about what was happening to his companions. A moment later, two more, one an officer, were captured.'

A German prisoner is directed back towards the Odon.

These Germans were the forward observation officers who had, in well-prepared and deep dugouts, called down fire on to their own positions. Thus hoping to drive off the increasing number of British who were arriving on the hill and occupying positions above them.

Despite losses of almost forty Shermans, the British position on Hill 112 was secure, as the infantry and tanks were joined by the all important supporting arms from divisional and corps troops. However, their positions on Hill 112 were surrounded on three sides and, in addition, they were at the end of a very exposed corridor, that was in places, little more than a mile wide! Lieutenant General O'Connor, commander VIII Corps, and Montgomery himself, must have been acutely aware of this as they digested the flash signal from Ultra: Rommel had authorized the release of the forty thousand men of II SS Panzer Corps. This powerful formation was to counter-attack the British salient from the west, astride the Odon, and destroy VIII Corps. Hill 112 and 11th Armoured Division in the bridgehead was under threat. Consequently, the most exposed elements of the division were withdrawn. Major Noel Bell of 8/RB describes the operation:

> 'There was much confusion. Nobody seemed to be sure what was happening or what the form was. Brian approached, supported under the arms by two of his section leaders. The parts of his face not covered with blood showed through deathly pale. We gave him a shot of brandy from a flask; he coughed. The trucks and carriers made their way back through the orchard. We saw a half-track burning, one of H Company's. Ammunition was exploding and the burning tyres made vivid circles of flames. We made lager, and attempted to find order out of chaos. A feeling of depression swept through us. There were only two officers left. The morning just a few hours behind us, seemed another age.'

The following morning, as the attack by II SS Panzer Corps was delayed until mid-morning, it seemed safe to order 3/RTR and their two companies of 8/RB back to Hill 112. They set off full of misgivings, anticipating another day under a continuous and heavy fire from the surrounding Germans. The enemy had, surprisingly, not reoccupied the hill, probably because the two SS Panzer Corps were concentrating on their part in the attack on the 'Scottish Corridor'. With little bother, 29 Armoured

Knocked out Shermans on Hill 112.

Brigade re-occupied their positions of the previous day on Hill 112. However, as Major Noel Bell recalled, all was not quiet for long:

> 'Shelling and mortaring commenced, varying in pitch from time to time. Bren carriers were blown bodily off the ground, but there were no direct hits. Our mortars, working with those of 'H' Company, put down a steady stream of fire. Sergeant Hollands continued to operate the mortars until wounded by shrapnel. Naish, leaning against a bank above his slit trench, was holding the wireless headphones in his hand, the better to hear any approaching shells, when there was an explosion nearby; shrapnel tore through the Bakelite, leaving in his hand only the metal band.'

Later in the day, a crisis was approaching as the German armour closed in on the Scottish Corridor. Everywhere the British were under pressure. In Montgomery's words:

> 'In view of this it was decided that VIII Corps should concentrate for the time being on holding the ground won, and regrouping started with the object of withdrawing the armour into reserve ready for new thrusts.'

This bland statement, with the safety of hindsight, belies the real gravity of the situation. Hill 112 had to be given up, as without 11th Armoured Division and the corps troops, who were urgently needed elsewhere, the hill could not be held. The 15th Scottish and 43rd Wessex Divisions were already fully committed to holding ground and could not spare any men to re-deploy to replace the armour that was being withdrawn in order to mount counter-attacks.

On Hill 112 Trooper John Thorpe recorded in his diary:

> *'Warning Order received: Abandon tanks after destroying gun. But no action until confirmed.*
>
> *New orders: Retreat, taking the tanks with us. Does anyone know what is going on?'*

Thus ended Operation EPSOM. With the historian's gift of hindsight, it is clear that those commanding the British battle had not fully appreciated the value of Hill 112. They were content to hold a shallow bridgehead over the Odon and give up the firm hold they had on Hill 112. As we shall see, this decision was to have tragic consequences for the soldiers who were to fight for its possession over the following month.

A section of the Rifle Brigade rest beside their half-track on the reverse slope of Hill 112.

CHAPTER TWO

PREPARATION FOR OPERATION JUPITER

A month after D-Day, the Allies had been able to ensure that their rate of build up of men and material had exceeded that of the Germans. They were relatively secure in their lodgement but space was limited, as some D-Day objectives had still not been taken. Caen, 3rd Division's D-Day objective, and Carpiquet airfield, to the west of the city, were still stubbornly held by the Germans. The severe Channel storm over the period 19-22 June, and the consequent destruction of the Americans' prefabricated Mulberry Harbour, had caused some delays to operations, as a result of a lack of supplies. It could be said that the Allies had won the 'break-in' or landing and build up phase but the breakout battle was still proving to be an open issue.

Montgomery's Plan

As Operation EPSOM wound down on 30 June 1944, Montgomery summarized the tactical situation and gave instructions to his two army commanders, Generals Bradley and Dempsey, in his Top Secret Directive M 505.

'The General Situation

1. My broad policy, once we had secured a firm lodgement area, has always been to draw the main enemy forces in to the battle on our eastern flank, and to fight them there, so that our affairs on the western [US Army] *flank could proceed the easier.*

2. We have been very successful in this policy. Cherbourg has fallen without any interference from enemy reserves brought in from other areas; the First US Army is proceeding with its re-organization and re-grouping, undisturbed by the enemy; the western flank is quiet.

All this is good; it is on the western flank that territorial gains are essential at this stage, as we require space on that side for the development of our administration.

By forcing the enemy to place the bulk of his strength in front of the Second Army, we have made easier the acquisition of territory on the western flank.

3. Our policy has been so successful that the Second Army is now opposed by a formidable array of German Panzer Divisions - eight definitely identified, and possibly more to come.

The more recent arrivals seem to have come from far afield. The Divisions identified between CAUMONT and CAEN are as follows:

21 PZ, 2 PZ, 1 SS, 2 SS, 9 SS, 10 SS, 12 SS, LEHR'

Although there were eight German panzer divisions facing the Second British Army, there were only the equivalent of two on the American front. However, back at SHAPE, Eisenhower and his staff did not entirely share Montgomery's positive view of the situation. Eisenhower had grudgingly, approved Montgomery's strategy after a briefing prior to D-Day, yet after the war he wrote:

'...I and all of my service commanders and staff were greatly concerned about this strategic situation near Caen. Every possible means of breaking the deadlock was considered and I repeatedly urged Montgomery to speed up and intensify his efforts to the limit. Montgomery threw in attack after attack...'

The US press was increasingly critical of the campaign's slow development, particularly on the British front. For obvious reasons, Montgomery was unable to defend himself from such criticism by making his strategy public.

Montgomery went on to give directions to his army commanders: Generals Dempsey and Bradley. The key directives were:

'6. Our tactics must remain unchanged. Briefly, they are as follows:

(a) To retain the initiative.

We shall do this only by offensive action. On no account must we remain inactive. Without the initiative we can not win... .

<u>*Second British Army*</u>

8. Tasks as follows:

(a) To hold the main enemy forces in the area between CAEN and VILLERS BOCAGE... .'

Hill 112 was a natural choice for one of the areas where 'offensive action' was to be maintained. The Official History describes Montgomery's operational aims, once Caen had fallen, as follows:

> '*Some days must elapse while troops were being regrouped for these twin attacks* [US attack towards St Lo and the British Operation GOODWOOD], *and meanwhile the pot was to be kept boiling by a limited action to hold the enemy armour in the east and to round off the ground won in the Epsom battle... .*'

Operations in the Hill 112 area were to be code-named Operation JUPITER and were to be undertaken by the greatly reinforced 43rd Wessex Division, under command of VIII Corps. After the event, Montgomery described his intentions to

> '*threaten to break out of the initial bridgehead on the eastern flank – that is, in the Caen sector. I intended by means of this threat to draw the main enemy reserves into that sector, to fight them there and keep them there, using the British and Canadian armies for the purpose.*'

Montgomery goes on, at uncharacteristic length, to justify his decision to commit a division to attack Hill 112. His reasons were in accordance with his overall strategy:

> '*Second Army had therefore to position itself for delivering a major thrust east of the Orne when the right time came; that would be when the American break-out operation had gathered momentum and was striking east.*
>
> '*There were other urgent reasons for wanting to develop a bridge head east of the Orne* [from the area of Hill 112] ... *First: we had to extend the bridgehead in order to gain space to manoeuvre; this could be achieved best by attacking from the existing bridgehead to the south, south-east and east. Secondly: we required a firm left flank, so that we could launch major attacks to the south without fear of becoming unbalanced by enemy action on our left rear....* [east of the Orne Canal and River]. *Thirdly: we required lateral east-west routes, which passed south of the Caen bottleneck. We should not achieve our object if we created a salient, south-east of Caen, and had to rely on maintenance routes which involved a long detour... it follows that we had to thrust south between the Odon and the Orne in order to open lateral routes to the west.*'

The German Situation and Plan

At the same time that Montgomery was writing his upbeat M 505 directive to his army commanders, *Generalfeldmarschal* Wilhelm Keitel was on the phone from Berlin to C-in-C West,

Generalfeldmarschall von Rundstedt. The conversation, recorded by Milton Shulman in his book *Defeat In The West*, went thus: Keitel: 'What shall we do?' von Rundstedt icily replied: 'What shall we do? What shall you do? Make peace you idiots! What else can you do?' With that he calmly hung up. Two days later von Rundstedt was relieved of his command.

Since well before D-Day the Germans had been victims of the deception-plan Operation FORTITUDE. The Allies' aim was to convince the enemy that the Normandy landings were a feint and that taking vital divisions away from the Pas de Calais would be a mistake. So successful was the deception, that not only did it ensure that the

Generalfeldmarschall Wilhelm Keitel.
'What shall we do...?'

initial build up outstripped the gradual release of German divisions from the Fifteenth Army, but also that the threat of the non-existent First US Army Group (FUSAG) was still believed a month after D Day. Indeed, the day the British launched their attack on Hill 112, 10 July 1944 – Rommel signalled C-in-C West:

'The enemy has at present 35 divisions in the landing area. In Great Britain another 60 Divisions may at any moment be transferred to the continent. We shall have to reckon with the large scale landing of 1 US Army Group in the north for strategic co-operation with the Montgomery Army Group in a thrust on Paris.'

Generalfeldmarschall Gerd von Rundstedt.
'Make peace you idiots!'

In fact, the phantom FUSAG only consisted of the charismatic General Patton, a handful of troops, some signals units, poorly-concealed blow-up rubber tanks and fake plywood landing craft. The Allies had yet another vital capability: Ultra. The Ultra code breakers at Bletchley Park had the ability to intercept and read German Enigma encoded radio communications. By 1944, use of Ultra intelligence was central to the Allies' conduct of the war. It enabled the Allies to reinforce the enemy's existing beliefs and manipulate their concerns to suit Allied purposes. The combination of Ultra (intelligence) and FORTITUDE (deception) gave the Allies the freedom to assemble sufficient troops at the right time, and in the right place, to ensure a prosperous campaign. On the other side, the Germans had barely sufficient resources available in Normandy to hold the Allies, let alone to 'throw them back into the sea' as Hitler demanded.

The arrival of II SS Panzer Corps from Russia at the end of June should have provided the Germans with a formation powerful enough to wrest some of the initiative from the Allies. The Corps, however, arrived at the height of Operation EPSOM and was fed piecemeal into battle. It successfully blunted the British attack, but shortage of troops in the face of relentless pressure and seemingly overwhelming material resources, condemned II SS Panzer Corps to holding a vital piece of ground: Hill 112. In all armies, tactical purists would have argued that a panzer division holding static positions was a criminal waste. Traditionally, the characteristics of armoured formations of mobility, protection and firepower are combined to achieve results through shock action, not through positional defence. Consequently, *Generalfeldmarschall* Rommel directed *Generaloberst* Eberbach, Commander Panzer Group West, to review the situation. Orders were given that 9th SS Panzer Division, holding the sector immediately to the west of Hill 112, was to be relieved by 277th Infantry Division from the Fifteenth Army at the pas de Calais. Making their way to Normandy was a slow process for the German infantry. Any movement by day was subject to Allied fighter-bomber attack and, lacking road or rail transport, the Division made their

Generalfeldmarschall Erwin Rommel.

journey largely on foot and mostly at night

Just before Operation JUPITER, the German aim had been to extract II SS Panzer Corps from defensive operations so that it could form the nucleus of an armoured reserve. As slow moving infantry divisions arrived in Normandy, German armour would be progressively freed from being forced to react to Allied moves and become, instead, a mobile striking force capable of dictating the course of events. As a first step in achieving this, 9th SS *Hohenstaufen* Panzer Division was to concentrate in hides to the south-west. Here it would be well placed to support either 10th SS *Frundsberg* Panzer Division, who were still in the line at Hill 112, or XLVII Panzer Corps. 9th SS Panzer Division started thinning out on the night of 7 July and moved to well-dispersed hides, with the Divisional Headquarters at Maisoncelles, to the south west of Villers Bocage. From here, the Division would be well placed to mount operations against either the Second British Army or the First US Army. Once out of the line, 9th SS Panzer Division's tank strength increased significantly, from on average 50 percent strength after two weeks of battle to approximately 75 percent. Repairs were carried out and such SS reinforcements as were available were taken in to the Division's battle-scarred

SS-*Oberführer* Heinz Harmel, Commander of 10th SS Panzer Division

units. The regeneration of 9th SS Panzer Division's combat power created a viable German armoured reserve; exactly what Montgomery was striving to prevent!

The rate of release and movement of German infantry divisions to Normandy meant that 10th *Frundsberg* SS Panzer Division was still needed to hold Hill 112. There is some debate as to whether or not the German commanders would have been happy to allow the key feature of Hill 112 to be held by a less powerful formation than an SS Panzer Division. However, as 43rd Wessex Division was to find out, the *Frundsberg* was still very firmly in position. The broad mass of Hill 112 was held by 21 SS Panzer Grenadier Regiment (the equivalent of a British

A German *Wehrmacht* lieutenant from an Assault Gun unit confers with men of *Waffen* SS unit during the fighting around Caen.

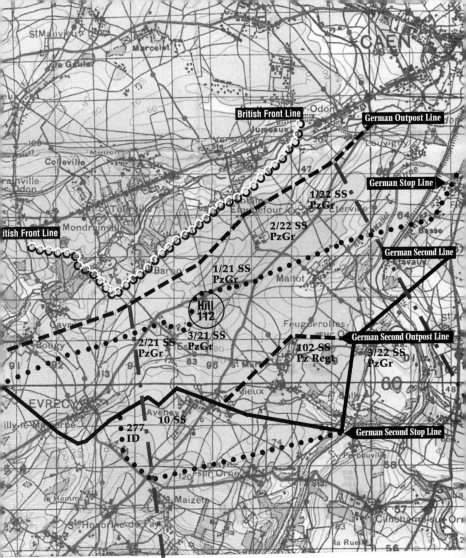

Operation JUPITER – The Battle area showing dispositions of units of the 10 SS Panzer Division around Hill 112, southwest of Caen.

brigade), while 22 SS Panzer Grenadiers held the narrow gap between the eastern edge of Hill 112 and the River Orne. Both regiments held the area with several defensive lines. The Division's reconnaissance and pioneer battalions occupied further in-depth positions that covered the Orne crossings. In support were not only the guns of 10th SS Artillery Regiment and II SS Panzer Corps, but also the much feared and loathed multi-barrelled rocket launchers (*nebelwerfers*) of 8 *Werfer* Brigade. The well dug-in SS soldiers, with their armoured reserves and impressive firepower, meant that the *Frundsberg*'s defences on Hill 112 were going to be a tough nut for 43rd Wessex Division to crack.

Operation JUPITER – Objectives

The man who commanded 43rd Wessex Division during its first offensive operation of the Normandy campaign was Major General Gwilym Ivo Thomas. He was renowned as an austere figure; respected rather than liked. Originally a Gunner officer, General Thomas had gained considerable experience during the First World War. In his three years at the front he took part in some of the hardest battles of the war. Rising to command a battery at twenty-three years of age, he won an MC and Bar, as well as a DSO. His experiences on the Western Front shaped his military philosophy and appreciation of the nature of war. In March 1942, following his appointment to command the almost exclusively Territorial Army 43rd Wessex Division, General Thomas completed its transformation from a coastal defensive formation into one of the best infantry divisions fighting in the North West European Campaign. He earned a reputation as a tough and innovative trainer of troops with very high standards. Little escaped his eye and he impressed on all those under his command, his intended tactical methods.

Despite his unconventional battle dress, highly polished riding boots and breeches General Thomas 'conceived warfare in terms of speed – speed of thought and decision – of rapid issue of orders and effective communication'. He was a tough and driving commander in battle. His aide-de-camp, Captain Pat Spencer-Moore, thought that 'Many officers feared a confrontation with the GOC more than they did the enemy!' Sharing a trait with many of history's successful commanders, he had a brutal streak and was prepared to commit troops to potentially costly operations. However, in common with most British commanders who had fought in the previous war, he did not squander lives needlessly. His nickname, 'Butcher Thomas', predated the casualties incurred in his Division's battles and had more to do with his character and the robust manner with which he dealt with those who displeased him. The words of Brigadier Carver, whose 4 Armoured Brigade came under his

Appdx 'A' to 7 Seaforth OO No.1.
(dated 9 July 44.)

LIST OF CODE WORDS.

1. **Place Names.**

ETERVILLE	9864	GLOUCESTER.
CHOI DE FONTAINE.	9763	STROUD.
LIEU DE LA FRANCE.	9963	EXETER.
MALTOT.	9862	BATH.
FEUGUEROLLES-SUR-ORNE	9961	CARDIFF.
BARON.	9462	TRURO
CRx DES FILANDRIER.	958619	WINCHESTER.
ESQUAY.	9460	BRISTOL.
EVRECY.	9259	PLYMOUTH.
ST MARTIN VIEUX.	9760	NEWPORT.
BULLY.	9959	TORQUAY.
AMAYE-SUR-ORNE.	9757	SWANSEA.

2. **43 Div SL.** — "OATS".

3. **43 Div Objectives.**

    1st Objective — BARLEY.

    2nd Objective — RYE.

    Final Line. — WHEAT.

4. **River Crossing Places.**

    (a) **River ODON.**

Crossing	951646		CANT I
"	956648		CANT II
"	962649	(br)	CARRIAGE I
"	970654	(br)	CARRIAGE II

    (b) **River ORNE.**

Crossing	973595	PENNY	1
"	996590		3
"	004589		4
"	013597		5
"	012609		6
"	003622		7
"	005646		8
"	016650		9

5. **46 Bde Code Words.**

    (a) Am ready to adv and carry out task — BACON (issued by Bns)

    (b) Commence on task. — EGGS (issued by Bde).

A Bren gun carrier of the 8/Middelsex Regiment crossing the Odon in 'Death Valley'.

command during Operation JUPITER, summarize the views of many. General Thomas was:

'*A small, fiery, very determined and grim gunner, without a spark of humour, he would bite the head off anyone who attempted to disagree with him or question his orders, as I was soon to find out.*'

Major General Thomas was given his orders almost a week before the attack on Hill 112. Operation JUPITER was effectively 'on call' as it was predicated on the capture of Carpiquet airfield and Caen, which the Canadians and 3rd

Division eventually captured on 9 July 1944. In the battle that followed, 43rd Wessex Division, in the Hill 112 area, were to be VIII Corps's 'main effort', with subsidiary attacks being mounted by 15th Scottish Division and the newly arrived 53rd Welsh Division. To the west, further limited attacks by XXX Corps were to be mounted by 50th, 49th and 59th Divisions.

In pursuance of Montgomery's objectives, 43rd Division's mission was to seize a bridgehead across the River Orne. In doing so, they would provide the Second British Army with a springboard to advance across the enticingly open country that lay beyond the river. In order to achieve this, the Division would have to take the dominating and well-defended bulk of Hill 112. Major General Thomas's plan was for 129 Brigade to clear Hill 112 and establish artillery observation posts on the crestline, before falling back to defensive positions along the line of the Caen – Evrecy road. Meanwhile, on 129 Brigade's left, 130 Brigade, was to clear the low ground. Both of these brigades were to be supported by Churchill tanks of 31 Tank Brigade and Crocodiles (flame throwing variants of the Churchill) from 141/RAC Regiment of 79th Armoured Division. 4 Armoured Brigade's Sherman tanks, with 214 Brigade mounted in Kangaroo armoured personnel carriers, were to secure the Orne crossings and form a bridgehead beyond. 46 Brigade (from 15th

Kangaroo personnel carrier.

Field Marshal Montgomery with Major General Thomas and his staff.

Operation JUPITER – The Plan – Phases 1 and 2.

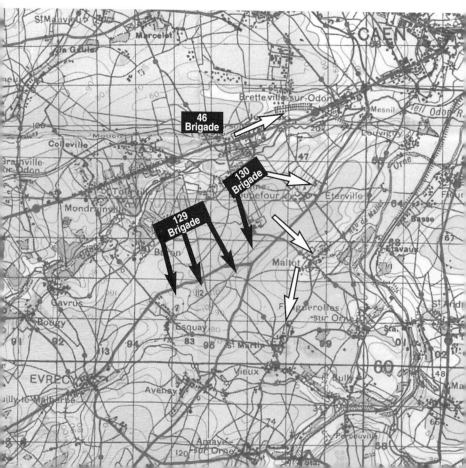

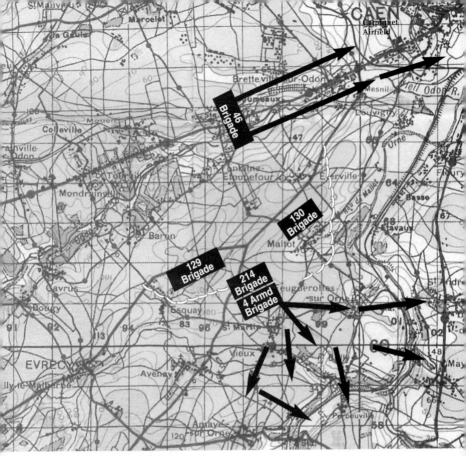

Operation JUPITER – The Plan – Phase 3.

Scottish Division) were to attack eastwards towards the southern suburbs of Caen.

The operation was to be conducted in three phases.

Phase 1. 130 Brigade, with 9/Royal Tank Regiment (RTR), were to clear a German salient in the area of les Duanes, which was held by a company of SS Panzer Grenadiers. Capture of Chateau de Fontaine, which was the location of battalion headquarters, 2/22 SS Panzer Grenadier Regiment, would follow. To their right, 129 Brigade, supported by 7/RTR, were to take the high ground of the Hill 112 feature.

Phase 2. 129 Brigade were to hold a defensive flank on Hill 112 facing south-west towards Evrecy on the northern slopes of the feature. 130 Brigade, supported by 9/RTR and Crocodiles, were to attack Eterville and Maltot. If possible, they were to follow up this success by advancing as far as the high ground to the south-east of Hill 112 in the direction of St Martin. Meanwhile, 46 Brigade and B Squadron 7/RTR were to provide left flank protection by taking over Verson and relieving 4/Dorsets in Eterville.

Phase 3. 129 Brigade was to continue to hold its positions on Hill 112, while 130 Brigade was to establish defences on a line Eterville – Maltot, facing the open flank to the east. At this stage, 4 Armoured Brigade and 214 Brigade were to be launched between 129 and 130 Brigades, south to the River Orne and, if the crossings were intact, form a bridgehead on the south-eastern bank. 46 Brigade, supported by B Squadron 7/RTR, were to clear the triangle of land on the left flank, between the Rivers Odon and Orne as far east as the suburbs of Caen.

Whatever the outcome of the attack on the morning of 10 July 1944, it was guaranteed that the Germans could not ignore the threat of the British armour securing a bridgehead on the open land beyond the River Orne. They would be bound to react to 43rd Wessex Division's attack with all means available.

10thSS *Frundsberg*
Panzer Division

43rd Wessex
InfantryDivision

CHAPTER THREE

OPERATION JUPITER
Assault on Hill 112

Pinning down exactly when various events happened on 10 July 1944 is difficult. Some primary sources, such as infantry war diaries, often written up some considerable time after the event, have all the inherent inaccuracies of recalled timings. However, more reliable are the diaries of the artillery, which were usually written in the relative safety of the gun position, some distance behind the frontline. These diaries are often supported by transcripts of the original signallers' radio and telephone logs, which give a feel for the information or often 'dissinformation' that contributes to 'the fog of war' so typical of battle. Also, of good quality are the diaries of armoured regiments where radio operators, in virtually every tank, were able to record much detail, in often wobbly writing, as the tank made its way across the shell pocked battlefield. Sergeant Trevor Greenwood of 15 Troop 9/RTR records in a personal diary, written in the turret of a Churchill tank, that 'time has no meaning during action: some time during the fight... The hours passed. Maybe two or three ...'. It seems that even the evidence

Often it was radio operators who recorded the accounts of the actions in their logs.

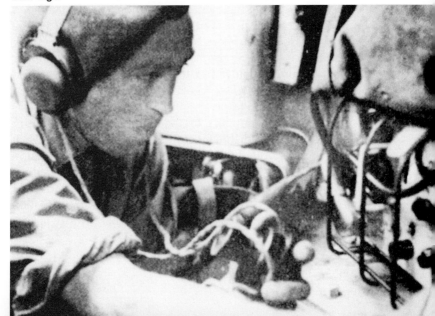

of contemporary documents has its limitations!

Some secondary sources, written after consulting British or German records, can add further confusion over timings of important events. For example the Germans were on Central European time, while the Allies were on Double British Summertime, which gives a time difference of two hours, not the normal one hour. Also, some commentators record attacks as taking place when they were ordered. This overlooks the fact that it takes considerable time for orders to be given and for infantry, moving at walking pace, to reach their Forming Up Places (FUP). This account of the battle attempts to reconcile the times and events from a whole range of sources.

The Bombardment

Captain DIM Robbins of 4/Wilts recalls:

'We were very well prepared for the battle. As I listened to the orders at 03.30 hours I thought that it was just like an exercise. We all knew exactly what to do. The orders were to cross the start line at 05.00 hours after a great barrage of artillery. We had a lot of guns by then from Corps and Army.'

At dawn (04.45 hours) 10 July 1944, the British opened the battle with a barrage of incredible intensity and for the fifteen minutes before H Hour, when the attacking British would rise out of the tall wheat and advance on Hill 112, the flashes of 1,000 guns cut the dawn sky.

Since 1941, the British Army had been increasing the strength of its artillery by raising new regiments and converting infantry battalions into gunner regiments. It was widely appreciated that the longer the campaign went on, the greater would be the demand for artillery support. In action on the Odon battlefield, the workhorse of the divisional artillery was the 25-pounder field gun. Mainly deployed in towed form, the gun was also mounted in self-propelled versions for use with armoured divisions. With a range of 13,400 yards, the 25-pounder was designed for close support to the fighting troops. Infantry divisions had an establishment of three artillery regiments. Each regiment was allocated to a brigade and each of the brigade's infantry battalions was supported by one of the regiment's three gun batteries. Every battalion, therefore, normally had eight guns allocated to its direct support. However, if the situation warranted they could 'lose' their guns to higher priority targets

A 25 pounder in action in Normandy, July 1944.

and it follows that fire from the rest of the regiment and, indeed, of the divisional artillery could be called on when needed. During Operation JUPITER the control of this flexible arrangement in 43rd Wessex Division, was via a shadow Royal Artillery command structure. At the lowest level a battery commander deployed with the infantry battalion's commanding officer, while up a level, the artillery regiment's commanding officer was closely linked to brigade headquarters. In overall control of the Division's guns was the CRA or Commander Royal Artillery, Brigadier Heath, who worked at divisional headquarters. He planned the artillery battle and ensured that priority targets received the appropriate weight of fire. Lieutenant Douglas Goddard (Gun Position Officer) recorded, in 220 Battery's war diary, the weight of fire available for divisional targets: 'Uncle target engaged. 1,260 rounds per minute for 19 mins'. For Operation JUPITER Brigadier Heath had under command a total of two hundred and sixty-four 25-pounders, including his own guns

Lieutenant Douglas Goddard

from 43rd Wessex Division and those from 11th Armoured, 15th Scottish, 53rd Welsh Divisions.

Also, committed to JUPITER, were the field, medium, heavy and super heavy guns of 3rd and 8th Army Groups Royal Artillery (AGRA). The AGRAs' main weapon was the 5.5in gun, which could hurl an eighty-pound shell 18,100 yards and, consequently, from their positions around Cheux, they could engage targets on the divisional objective and beyond without having to move. The only problem was having an observer able to identify targets and correct fire so deep in the enemy position. Possession of Hill 112 would give Royal Artillery Forward Observation Officers just such a position and it was worth fighting for!

At 22,000 yards from Sword Beach, the Royal Navy

A 5.5 inch gun in action around dawn. Note the impressive pile of shells, most of which would be fired in support of a major attack.

Bombardment Force could engage targets on Hill 112 with their guns, which ranged in calibre from 6 in to the massive 16 in guns mounted on HMS *Rodney*. Her nine guns fired shells weighing 2,641 pounds out to 38,000 yards with considerable accuracy but, carrying only a hundred rounds per gun, she could only be tasked to engage targets of the highest priority. However, the 'throw weight' of the naval bombardment force's broadside, which included the cruisers HMS *Roberts* and *Belfast*, considerably enhanced the fire available on the morning of 10 July 1944.

A paragraph from the divisional operation order summed up the artillery fire plan:

> **Arty SP.** *The initial attack on the first objective is covered by a 3,500 yd barrage at a gun to 35 yds. This barrage overlaps the flanks by 500 yds. It is backed by heavy concentrations from AGRA on all known centres of enemy resistance, eg les Duanes 9664, and is superimposed on the air programme. Counter bty* [battery] *and counter mortar from ZERO minus 60 to ZERO...Very hy* [heavy] *3" and 4.2" mortar concs* [concentrations] *are welded into the arty programme.*

From 220 Battery's gun position near St Manvieu (7,000 yards from Hill 112), Lieutenant Douglas Goddard recorded in his Battery's war diary the firing of the opening barrage:

> *'The entire Corps Arty engaged at rates of up to 5 RPM* [rounds not revolutions per minute] *with the guns having to be cooled with water.'*

The weight of fire from the massed artillery stunned the *Frundsberg's* Grenadiers, even in their well-prepared deep dugouts. Fire directed on the division's initial objectives on Hill 112 and the low ground to the east, was extremely accurate. The effect of the artillery on targets in depth was, however, less dramatic, as unobserved fire missions, taken off the map, tended to be less accurate due to the inability to correct fall of shot directly onto the target. For most Germans, the weight of British artillery fire was remarkable and Gunter Balko, an infantryman from 21 SS Panzer Grenadier Regiment, described the effect of shellfire on the individual:

> *'At Tarnopol we endure*[d] *heavy Russian artillery fire but in Normandy we were hit again and again, day after day by British artillery that was so heavy the Frundsberg bled to death before our eyes. It was worst during an attack, theirs or ours,*

les Duanes

Line of Advance

View from 5/Dorset's Forward Observation Post in Fontaine Etoupefour Church tower, 10 July 1944.

when we would be terribly blasted. I saw grenadiers struck dumb and unable to move and others made mad by the unceasing 'drumfire'. Your artillery is my worst memory of Normandy.'

Back in the *Frundsberg's* divisional headquarters the Chief of Staff, SS-*Hauptsturmführer* Klapdor, recalls:

'The telephone rang and a voice announced that "The enemy are firing smoke". This message was soon confirmed and completed from other sectors. Suddenly all hell lets loose. The front rumbles and the earth trembles and vibrates. The radio operator who is now awake, tries to establish contact with the units in the front line. Very nervously, he announces "All communication with the front is cut". We are all at once isolated. While we are thinking about what it is like at the front all of a sudden it was our turn. The enemy bombards the whole region, targeting woods, junctions and known positions. Hundreds of explosions tear the night.'

At 05.00 hours, as the barrage reached its peak, four infantry battalions rose from the shelter of their shell scrapes and advanced up the slopes of Hill 112. They moved through the waist high wheat towards the clouds of dust thrown up by the

Hill 112

Site of modern roundabout

Waffen SS Officers pictured during the fighting round Caen.

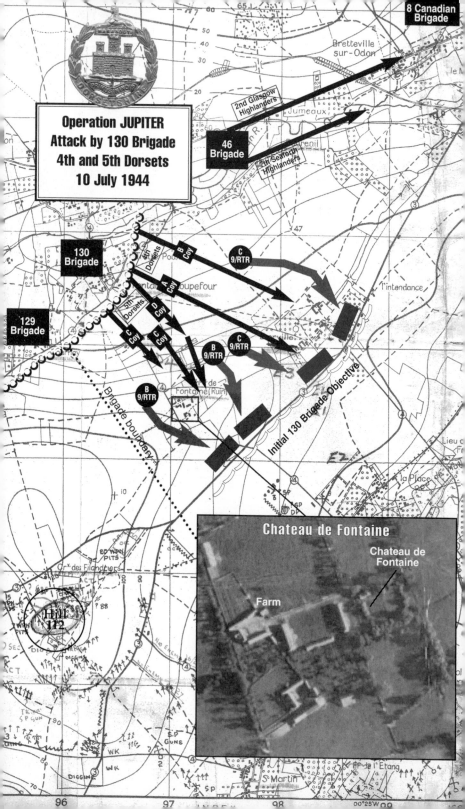

Operation JUPITER
Attack by 130 Brigade
4th and 5th Dorsets
10 July 1944

8 Canadian Brigade

Bretteville sur-Odon

2nd Glasgow Highlanders

46 Brigade

7th Seaforth Highlanders

l'Intendance

130 Brigade

4th Dorsets

B Coy

C 9/RTR

A Coy

5th Dorsets

D Coy

129 Brigade

C Coy

C Coy

C 9/RTR

B 9/RTR

Fontaine (Ruin)

B 9/RTR

Initial 130 Brigade Objective

Brigade boundary

Lieu

la Place

Hill 112

St Martin

Chateau de Fontaine

Chateau de Fontaine

Farm

96   97   98   00°25'W

5/Dorsets advance through fields of corn towards their objective.

exploding shells, that shrouded their objectives.

130 Brigade's Attack

On the extreme left of the tight Odon Bridgehead 5/Dorsets shook out into their assault formations. Their FUP was in the valley, out of sight of the enemy, just to the south of the village of Fontaine Etoupefour. Here *Nebelwerfers*, engaging all likely British positions in the valley below, inflicted the Dorset's first casualties of the day.

5/Dorsets were the leading troops of 130 Brigade's attack into the depths of the German defences on the low ground to the east of Hill 112. Their first objective was a German salient centred on the les Duanes farm complex. 7 Company, 2/22 SS Panzer Grenadier Regiment held the stoutly built stone farm-buildings, which they had developed into the central feature of a forward strong point. Little more than 400 metres from the Dorset's start line, the farm received particular attention from the heavy artillery. C Company, with two troops of Churchills from B Squadron 9/RTR, were quickly on the enemy position and found the enemy stunned by the ferocity of the barrage. Just ten minutes after H Hour, the Commanding Officer, Lieutenant Colonel Coad, waiting with the reserve sections,

> '...saw the green flare indicating success, rising from the smoke of the smouldering barns. It was with a feeling of relief that the battle had begun well for us, that I started to follow up with my reserve companies [A and B].'

Meanwhile, C Company's two erstwhile leading platoons sent sullen SS prisoners to the rear and prepared to follow the advance as company reserve. They formed up behind the two fresh platoons who had 'leapfrogged' through to take the lead. A Company, arriving at the farm, cleared the captured buildings, enemy trenches and bunkers in detail.

On 5/Dorset's left, D Company, with a single troop of Churchills, had further to advance to reach their objective at 'Horseshoe Wood'; so named because of its shape on the map. The battle here was to be considerably stiffer than at les Duanes, as the Germans had vital minutes to recover from the shock of the barrage and Horseshoe Wood was also a part of 2/22 SS Panzer Grenadier's main defensive position, held by outposts of 5 Company. D Company's momentum carried them onto the enemy trenches where the West Countrymen had their first experience of hand to hand fighting. Lieutenant Colonel Coad recalled that:

> 'Winkling out the loathsome SS with rifle butt, bullet and bayonet had been a costly affair. The evidence of D Company's fight lay all around me when I arrived with Advanced Battalion Headquarters some minutes later. Amongst the casualties was the company commander, Major Roe, and it would appear that Lieutenant Hayes had led his platoon too far towards the Chateau and was "lost". We subsequently discovered that they had all been killed or captured before C Company arrived in the area.'

Back on 5/Dorset's right flank, having taken les Duanes, C Company's main objective was the ancient and now shell-scarred ruins of Chateau de Fontaine. The barn between the Chateau and the farm complex near the road was SS-*Sturmbannführer* Loffler's headquarters of 2/22 SS Panzer Grenadiers. The defended chateau and farm was a tough nut for two companies to crack, as they were held by 2/22 SS's 6 Company, along with the heavy weapons of 8 Company. The Dorset's number 18 radio set had been badly damaged by a

5/ Dorset

les Duanes

Horseshoe Wood

D Coy

Coy

Eterville

North

HQ
2/22 SS
PzGr

Chateau
Fontaine

Hill 112

Maltot

les Duanes

Chateau de
Fontaine

A view back towards 'Death Valley' (River Odon) from Horseshoe wood looking
north across the ground D Company crossed.

shell splinter, just as C Company resumed the advance towards the Chateau and consequently, no word of their progress reached Battalion Headquarters. The first news of the Company's progress eventually reached the Commanding Officer via A Company, who reported that 'C is in difficulty on the northern edge of their objective'. Breaking into the SS defences was difficult and time consuming despite artillery firing in support. But the Dorsets were not the only ones in difficulty. SS-*Sturmbannführer* Hans Loffler recalls that:

'The telephone lines were cut and it was impossible to repair them in the enemy fire. The curtain of fire hit the CP and prevented all forms of communication. I knew that the position must be held. I decided to join the combat with a few men from the headquarters against the enemy who had penetrated through the advanced positions. I filled my camouflage jacket with grenades and took my rifle. I sprung out with my men but I had only been out a short time when a shell landed near me and cut into my leg. I was down and carried to the aid post of 1/22 SS Panzer Grenadier Regiment. The men carrying me had to fight their way through an enemy attack with pistol and grenade. I was wounded again by an exploding grenade...'

SS-*Sturmbannführer* Hans Loffler Commander Officer 2/22 Panzer Grenadiers.

Once the Dorsets were in the heart of the enemy defences, clearing the Chateau's buildings and barns seemed to consume men, but the companies continued to move slowly forward and eventually they occupied the whole area. As Lieutenant Colonel Coad could not get through on the radio, he moved from Horseshoe Wood to the Chateau to find out what was happening and influence the action at the nub of the battle. Here he met Major Newton at 05.52 hours, who confirmed that his company had just overrun the enemy position. 130 Brigade's signals log records a message received from Advanced Battalion Headquarters 5/Dorsets at '06.15 hrs. Chateau de Fontaine

A view of the Chateau de Fontaine, barn and farm complex from the south.

taken'. C Company was to find out that there was a world of difference between 'taking' a position and finally securing it, while under increasingly heavy artillery and mortar fire.

7/Somerset LI

As 5/Dorsets were to subsequently continue 130 Brigade's advance in support of 7/Hampshires they were relieved by 7/Somerset LI. The Somersets were faced with dealing with determined SS soldiers who had hidden themselves away and were sniping at the 'Wicked Wyverns' as they dashed from cover to cover. Although not taking part in the actual attack, 7/Somerset LI had had a hard time at Chateau de Fontaine. Their history records:

'Mortar and shellfire was devastating. Colonel Lance was killed by a shell from an 88, while sitting in his jeep, the Gunner Battery Commander, Major Mapp, was killed, the Adjutant, Capt. A. Scannell, was wounded and evacuated; a steady stream of wounded was arriving at the Regimental Aid Post. Major Young and Major Chalmers shared command of the battalion with that of their companies. Snipers were at their worst. Shortly after Colonel Lance was killed, Major Young's company was clearing some farm buildings at Chateau Fontaine. A shot whistled unpleasantly close and the Major turned to Pte. Lance (battalion sniper) who was with him 'That's the fifth shot that basket has fired at me, we must get him'. They found him hidden in a junk heap in the middle of the duck pond. They found another, he could not have been more than seventeen years old, who had buried himself in the mud of a wet ditch - only his head, arms and rifle were free and even these he had covered with slime and weeds. Another was burned out from a hayrick set on fire by a German shell. Several days after occupation of Chateau Fontaine snipers were

A *Waffen* SS man killed during the fighting around Caen.

still being found... . Enemy trenches in the area were full of German dead passed over by the leading troops, the usual scene of mutilated farm animals was all around. The air was rancid with the smell of dead animals and flies.'

As the final part of 130 Brigade's first attack of the day, C and D Companies of 5/Dorset, both pushed one of their reserve platoons forward with tanks of B Squadron. The reserve infantry and the comfortingly bulky Churchills took up exposed positions on the main Caen to Evrecy road. From here, they would be able to support further attacks into the heart of the German defences.

Ejected from their defensive positions around the Chateau, German infantry from 2/22 SS Panzer Grenadiers withdrew towards the relative safety of their 1st Battalion in Eterville. SS-*Hauptsturmführer* Richter commanding the 1st Battalion, recalls the severely wounded SS-*Sturmbannführer* Loffler, carried by grenadiers from Chateau Fontaine, who

SS-*Hauptsturmführer* Richter

deliriously cried 'Richter – Richter – Save my Battalion – Save my Battalion'. Richter was, however, about to face his own problems in Eterville.

While C Company 5/Dorset was still securing Chateau de Fontaine, at 06.20 hours 4/Dorsets started to advance on Eterville. The village was less than 700 metres from Horseshoe Wood, with a lane running north-south dividing it in two. To the west, the village's main feature was the eighteenth century chateau and large farm complex. To the east of the road was another large farm and spread around the whole village were smaller dwellings, trees and cider orchards. 1/22 Panzer Grenadier Regiment held Eterville along with a company of SS engineers acting as infantry. The remains of 1 SS (*Leibstandarte Adolf Hitler*) Panzer Grenadiers were dug in on the ridge that extended from the village in a north-easterly direction towards Louvigny.

Major Symonds wrote of the attack:

'B Company [left], *which I was commanding, was supported by a squadron of Churchill tanks* [C Squadron 9/RTR] *and A Company* [on the right] *by a troop of flame-throwers* [Crocodiles of 141/RAC, 79th Armoured Division].

'We formed up immediately behind the start line in a cornfield and were shelled a little while doing so, causing one or two minor casualties. [Lieutenant] Colonel Cowie gave the long awaited signal to go by having L/Cpl Butt sound the charge on

Tactical HQ 4/Dorsets moves up behind the assaulting companies towards Eterville.

his bugle. The Battalion rose to its feet as one man, many cheered. It was a wonderful moment to be there.

'As we breasted the top of the hill, we over-ran a German platoon [the outpost line] *immediately in front of my company. They offered practically no resistance, surrendering immediately, and we continued the advance to the edge of the village, where we had to lie down and wait for the artillery and RAF* [Typhoons] *to stop shelling and bombing Eterville. We were very close to the barrage, and still in excellent formation, having suffered only a few casualties from enemy shelling during the advance up to this time.*

'*The end of the supporting fire* [which included fire from 5/Dorset and B Squadron 9/RTR in Horseshoe Wood] *was marked by blue smoke shells, and I gave the signal to assault as soon as these fell. No sooner had we begun the assault than about four fighters came over, presumably a little late, and dropped two of their bombs in the middle of my company whilst we were still in the open field. We could see the bombs falling so had time to take cover, but we suffered a number of casualties including Sgt Fowler who was killed.*'

The Churchills of C Squadron 9/RTR were leading the infantry towards Eterville and Sergeant Trevor Greenwood, then a troop

sergeant, wrote:

'Every fibre of my being was concentrated on one thing – enemy gun flashes – miss them and there may not be a second chance. Most observation was done thro' the periscopes: too much machine-gunning over the top. Closed down occasionally when mortars became too concentrated around us.

'We reached the crest... And there were the enemy running for cover... towards Eterville and reached the trees ahead. Our Besa [coaxial mounted machine gun] *opened up... every bush and shrub: every tree: every haystack: anything and everything that could hide a body... was raked with machine-gun fire.*

'Our infantry were now among and ahead of us... and soon, prisoners started to come in: odd couples of Jerrys popping up from the corn, hands raised... scared to death... Very soon, we opened up with HE on the village... there were as yet no signs of any 88s. The infantry kept steadily on... walking warily through the deep corn, but always going forward... forward. Our Besa fire passed over them, but it must have been uncomfortably close. Grand fellows those infantry lads: so brave and calm.'

The pattern of the advance for the Crocodiles, flame-throwing variants of the Churchill, from 141/RAC Regiment was the same except, rather than engaging with HE and machine-gun fire, they aimed to burn the enemy out of his positions. Private Alfie Brown of A Company, on 4/Dorsets' right, was sheltering somewhat hesitantly behind the bulk of the Crocodiles fuel trailer as they advanced within a hundred metres of the edge of the village,

'...when there was a rushing sound like a train and a loud wumf as the hedge caught fire... black oily smoke was everywhere. I don't know if any Jerrys were caught but I saw some further along, running back from bunkers to the mansion. As a result, we got into Eterville fairly easily but that's when our problems really began ... .'

Infantry positions were not the only ones taken on by the Crocodiles. SS *Mann* August Bauer, a member of the 8 Company 2/22 Panzer Grenadiers, who crewed a gun mounted on a half track, recalls an incident between Chateau de Fontaine and Eterville:

'We shot at the advancing tanks with everything we had. Suddenly a great cloud of black smoke emanated from an armoured flame thrower and hit the cannon of SS-Rottenführer

Theopil Hauth situated to our right. The cannon was put out of action and the commander and crew were killed or wounded. We knocked out several English tanks before we were forced back into the village.' [Eterville]

Having 'got the infantry into the village' the Crocodiles withdrew to refill their 400-gallon flame fuel tanks, while C Squadron turned its attention to the open, eastern or left flank. They avoided the close country of Eterville, where they would have been vulnerable to the enemy's short range, hand held, anti-tank weapon, the *Panzerfaust*. Outside the village, the divisional artillery laid and maintained a smoke screen for four hours to cover the open left flank of the advance. This was just as well for 9/RTR, as the remnants of 1st (*Leibstandarte Adolf Hitler*) and 12th (*Hitler Jugend*) SS Panzer Divisions had concentrated in the area after their ejection from Caen in the preceding days. But for the smoke, a mixed bag of about seventy Mark IVs, Panther tanks and assault guns could have inflicted terrible damage on 130 Brigade. Some of these tanks patrolling the road from Louvigny to Maltot, were the Panzer IVs of the *Hitler Jugend*'s No 5 Company, 2/12 SS Panzer Regiment, commanded by *SS-Obersturmführer* Willi Kandler. Ignoring his divisional boundary and instructions, he probed forward

A knocked out MkIV on the outskirts of Eterville.

through the billowing smoke towards Eterville and

> *'engaged and destroyed a small English open-topped tracked*
> *vehicle dashing along the road in front of me. Their infantry*
> *were already attacking the Chateau. I withdrew to report.'*

His report confirmed what both I and II SS Panzer Corps already knew, that 10th SS Panzer Division was under heavy attack.

Once in the village the 4/Dorsets' plan was for the leading companies (A and B) to fight through Eterville quickly and reach their objective, the main road at the southern edge of the village. Again, detailed clearance was the task of the reserve companies and these were to be followed at 08.00 hours by 9/Cameronians who were to relieve 4/Dorsets and take over defence of the village.

Initially, the battle went according to plan for the Dorsets but for the Germans things were not going so well. Just before 07.00 hours *SS-Rottenführer* Schwingle burst into his Battalion's headquarters towards the rear of the village shouting 'Forward companies taken prisoner. Engländer 200 metres away with small tracked vehicles and infantry'. A few minutes later at 07.00 hours, 10th SS Panzer Division soberly reported to their Corps Headquarters that 'forward companies of 1/22 SS Panzer Grenadiers overrun in Eterville'.

Attacking on a two-company frontage, 4/Dorsets found that after breaking into the village A and B companies started to diverge left and right, as the two rifle companies were drawn towards enemy strong points. Advanced Battalion Headquarters, unusually, found itself in the front-line, acting as a link between the companies. In the centre, Corporal Chris Portway, a twenty-one year old section commander, found himself

> *'on my own in the churchyard with two Germans. They*
> *dashed from gravestone to gravestone with me firing at them.*
> *Eventually they got into the church where I got them with a*
> *grenade.'*

Shortly afterwards, he met the Commanding Officer who had just arrived in the midst of the confused fighting in the village. Corporal Portway was not impressed to be asked in a somewhat helpless manner 'What's happening, Corporal?' With the Commanding Officer and Advance Battalion Headquarters was Sergeant Geoff Cleal, the Battalion's Chief Clerk:

The Farm in the eastern part of Etervile in B Company, 4/Dorsets area.

Entrance to Eterville Church where Tactical HQ 4/Dorsets was located.

Chateau de Eterville today. During the battle the roof bore a white square with a red cross painted on it.

CO's carrier

Sgt Cleal's trench

Eterville today looking from the church towards the centre of the village.

'As we arrived beside the church we were greeted by a barrage of shells. The thick walls surrounding the churchyard seemed to bounce outwards and then fall back into place. The church became the Regimental Aid Post. Dug in tanks continued to pump shells into it killing wounded as they lay on their stretchers. Outside I recall two of us digging in Battalion Headquarters in front of the churchyard wall but behind a tree, with the idea that each of us could lean on the tree to fire our rifles. The CO was about twenty yards away directing operations over the R/T from his carrier. On the left, two other Bren gun carriers were on fire and ammunition in them was exploding every few seconds. My mate and I must have had charmed lives because shells were going through the wall behind us and one actually hit the tree above us. Suddenly my mate shouted, 'I've been hit'. 'Where?' I enquired. 'In the ass' came the reply! Turning him around and carrying out a hasty inspection, I recall saying 'I can't see any blood, forget it. We've got to finish digging this bloody hole'. Some twenty-four hectic hours later, still complaining, I got him to take down his trousers! To my astonishment, the whole of his bum and top of one leg was black and blue.'

Eventually A and B Companies pushed on ahead of Battalion Headquarters. A Company, who had cleared the Eterville Chateau, found that they had captured 2/22 SS Panzer Grenadiers aid post with sixty wounded. SS-*Hauptsturmführer* Richter describes the action:

'I told the doctor that he would have to stay with the wounded as the English would not be able to look after them during the fighting. Leaving the Chateau we took up positions at the rear edge of the village in a ditch by the edge of the road. Many had already retreated from the village to join the Battalion reserve. We held this position for about two hours. We only had three light machineguns and rifles. We let the English infantry advance to within thirty metres. As they came through the long grass, we opened fire. They were all downed without exception. After this we were not under fire for a short time and we were free to disengage to the rear. Two enemy machineguns advanced from the Chateau but we had a head start and successfully retreated 1,000 metres towards the bend in the Orne. On the way back we were joined by stragglers from the Leibstandarte [who had been holding the eastern edge of Eterville] and we soon numbered sixty five.'

A section from one of 4/Dorsets reserve companies await the call to move forward.

The SS Doctor, Moeferdt, had a hard time persuading his excited captors from A Company 4/Dorsets that he and his medics should be allowed to stay and treat the German wounded. After a terse discussion during which he quoted the Geneva convention he was allowed to stay. The wounded, who included SS *Sturmbannführer* Loffler, were hoping that they would be released by counter-attackers from the divisional reserve. No counter-attack reached the wounded SS soldiers, who were evacuated as prisoners of war in Bren gun carriers.

By 07.45 hours, 4/Dorsets were reporting that they had reached their objective and that Eterville was occupied. In reality, however, the battle in and around the village was to go on all day and into the following night. Major Symonds continued his account:

'We... reached our objectives... without too much difficulty. A

number of Germans surrendered, some withdrew, and some had yet to be mopped up. The mopping up was done by C and D Companies, which was not so easy, as the garden and field hedges were high and the foliage thick, and soon enemy troops, who had been quiet to start with, opened fire on us. The enemy then began to shell and mortar us very heavily, and he kept this up all the time we were consolidating, making the whole job very difficult.'

This account's understatement is revealed by the Dorset's casualties in Eterville and by the fact that its author, Major Symonds, was himself wounded during the consolidation phase and awarded the Military Cross. His was not to be the only MC awarded to this Battalion in Eterville.

As soon as it became apparent that the enemy had secured a foothold in Eterville, Grenadiers of 12th (*Hitler Jugend*) SS Panzer Division, in reserve in the woods to the east of Maltot, immediately counter-attacked. This was standard German practice but hastily attacking into a fluid battle, their advance soon lost momentum amongst the hedges and buildings of Eterville. SS-*Mann* Zimmer was with them:

'...Tommy attacks with great masses of infantry and many tanks. We fight as long as possible but we realize that we are in a losing position. By the time the survivors try to pull back, we realize that we are surrounded. In our sector, we have been driven back by the British infantry attack and they had bypassed us to left and right. I moved as fast as I could under the continuous firing. Others who tried to do the same failed. When the small-

Grenadiers of the *Hitler Jugend* during the Normandy fighting.

arms stopped our own guns got going. I lay there in the midst of it all. I still can't understand how I escaped, with... shell splinters tearing around my ears... Suddenly three Tommies appeared and they took me prisoner. Immediately I was given a drink and a cigarette. At the concentration point for prisoners I met my Unter-scharführer [SS Sergeant] and other comrades belonging to my company....'

SS-*Mann* Zimmer was lucky to survive the battle unwounded. Others on both sides were not so lucky. The situation in 4/Dorsets' Regimental Aid Post at the church was dire. The number of Dorset casualties would have overwhelmed the RAP staff and the attached RAMC field ambulance section on their own but there were also an almost equal number of wounded SS soldiers needing treatment. The Padre courageously went forward towards the enemy position under a flag of truce to find German medical personnel to help. Together the SS and British medics worked to treat casualties of both sides, all the while under fire and in danger from falling masonry, as the

A Field Dressing Station in the Odon Valley region where the wounded of both sides were treated.

shells gradually reduced the church to a ruin. Soon the RAP was overflowing with casualties, and soldiers of both sides were being wounded for a second time while they lay on their stretchers in the churchyard awaiting treatment or evacuation. Seldom have medics had to fight their battle to save comrades' lives in such harrowing circumstances. Soldiers and medics from both sides, who had worked together for many hours on that day, are on record as having expressed mutual respect for their opposite numbers' professionalism and impartiality. For his courage under fire and for his personal example and leadership, the Battalion Medical Officer, Captain Thompson, earned a very well-deserved Military Cross.

In the open country beyond Eterville and its surrounding orchards, the tanks of C Squadron 9/RTR were watching the open flanks. On call just behind them, were the M10 tank destroyers from 129 Battery, 86th (5th Devons) Anti-Tank Regiment RA. The RTR's Churchills were heavily armoured; however they only mounted a 75mm gun, which was inadequate in a tank to tank duel with all but the oldest German panzers. The M10 on the other hand mounted a 17-pounder gun, which was arguably the best Allied anti-tank gun of the war, but they were lightly armoured and consequently had to keep out of danger. Sergeant Jim Stephens of E Troop explained:

'The plan was that our self propelled 17-pounders were to advance and give protection to the Churchills, who were completely and always outgunned by the German 88s. Our 17-pounders would even things up – in theory!'

Having spent three years training to defend captured ground, an impromptu change to an offensive role that they were neither trained nor equipped to perform, did not impress Sergeant Stephens. Surely a tank to match the Panther and Tiger in its own right would have been better?

'E Troop moved out with C Squadron 9/RTR to support 4/Dorsets to attack Eterville, which was soon taken. We were called up to shoot up houses from the outskirts of the village that were holding the enemy; taking out OPs and machine gun nests.'

The disadvantage of the M10 was that the turret top was a five-foot open square. During the morning, in a forward position on the objective south of Eterville ...

'One M10 had a mortar bomb drop straight into it killing

instantly the Number 1 Sergeant, the gunner and loader ... The
Wireless operator and driver were badly burnt but managed to
bale out and make it back to the RAP.'

Another M10 was knocked out of action by an airburst shell that
wounded virtually all the crew before they had even seen an
enemy tank.

The attack on Eterville had gone well. The objective was
reached on time but the German response of shelling and
counter-attacks had slowed the progress of detailed clearance
and consolidation. In addition, Headquarters 130 Brigade had
underestimated the amount of time that even the well-trained
4/Dorsets would need in practice, to clear a real enemy out of a
built up area. The Division's inexperience was showing. The
main problem was that the strongpoints that had been
bypassed, needed clearing by the follow up companies who had
little idea of where it was safe to move and which areas were
still covered by enemy fire. In the village, equally determined
West Country and SS infantrymen fought a bitter struggle for
each room of every building. Casualties mounted quickly on
both sides.

9/Cameronians followed 130 Brigade out of the Odon valley
with orders to relieve 4/Dorsets as soon as they had taken the
village of Eterville. The regimental history describes the
situation:

'Lieutenant Colonel Villiers halted the Cameronians in
Fontaine Etoupefour, about 1,000 yards from Eterville, while he
went forward to contact the 4th Dorsets. On arrival at Eterville
he found it a most uninviting spot. It is a large straggling
village, much overgrown with trees and orchards. There was
practically no observation. The only approach for vehicles was by
a sunken lane, which at the time was blocked by several of the
Dorsets' carriers, all of which were in flames. The Dorsets were
still fighting for possession of the far side of the village itself,
which was being continually mortared by the enemy. As a
defensive position Eterville was a tactical nightmare. Lieutenant
Colonel Villiers decided none the less that the Cameronians must
start taking over immediately in order to relieve the Dorsets for
their next operation.'

The Cameronians were about to undertake one of the most
complicated operations in warfare; a relief in place while in
contact with the enemy. The relief was to be made that much

The M10, with its 17-pounder gun, could take on the German Panthers and Tigers but, because of its relatively light armour and open turret, its crews had to exercise extreme caution.

more difficult as the Cameronians had immediately to defend the village, without the benefit of recconnisance. Positions chosen from maps and air photos before the operation proved to be unsuitable as the thick hedges and trees denied the Highlanders a decent field of fire. To the tremendous credit of this battalion, they had relieved 4/Dorsets by midday allowing the Dorsets to concentrate, by 13.00 hours, as 130 Brigade reserve located near Horseshoe Wood. Wounded Scotsmen, mainly hit by mortar fire, started to join the West Countrymen in the RAP at the church. C Company 9/Cameronians took up position in a wooded part of the village centre and the other three rifle companies were completing the trenches begun by the Dorsets. The soundness of these defensive positions was to be fully tested before the end of the day.

The original plan was that by mid morning 4/Dorsets, as brigade reserve, were to have moved up behind 7/Hampshires. If they had been immediately available, as planned, to confirm

Attacking across the Odon River.

and exploit 7/Hampshire's success, the day may have turned out differently. But that is anticipating events.

129 Brigade's attack on Hill 112

While 130 Brigade was preparing the way for 4 Armoured Brigade's exploitation to the Orne between Hill 112 and the river, 129 Brigade was to advance on a broad front. Its objective was the key ground (to both sides) of Hill 112. To take the feature, 129 Brigade was to attack simultaneously with all three of its battalions, supported by two squadrons of 7/RTR and Crocodiles of 79th Armoured Division. Their task was different from that of 130 Brigade, in that there were no villages to be taken, just the broad open slopes of Hill 112 that rose gently from the restricted Odon valley. On the left, alongside 5/Dorsets at Chateau de Fontaine, were 4th Battalion, The Wiltshire Regiment (4/Wilts) and in the centre was 4th Battalion, The Somerset Light Infantry (4/Somerset LI), who had the task of taking point 112. The Brigade's third battalion, 5/Wilts, was on the right with the task of capturing the slopes between Hill 112 and the hamlet of le Bon Repos. 129 Brigade's plan was for the three battalions to take the Eterville to Evrecy road as their initial objective and, in a second phase, clear the ridgeline. Having taken the feature, they were to establish observation posts and battle outposts before falling back to a defensive

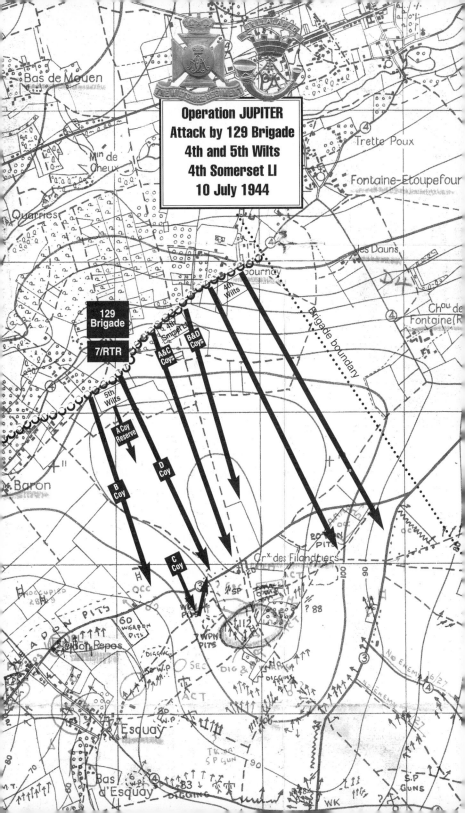

position on the rear slope of the Hill. H Hour for the attack was, as with 130 Brigade, 05.00 hours.

4/Wilts

Things started to go badly for 4/Wilts before the attack had even started. Captain DIM Robbins MC of B Company recalls the inauspicious start to the day:

Captain DIM Robbins MC

> 'We lined up in the open in the FUP and over zoomed the artillery. It was very noisy and quite exciting. Suddenly some heavier artillery started coming whistling towards us like a train. I thought that this was unusual and that it may land near us and it surely did. It was our 5.5 inch medium guns dropping short. They wrote off our leading platoon. I remember men from 11 Platoon lying all over the place and one chap being carted off in a wheelbarrow with no legs. The company commander said 'We can't go into battle with the SS like this'. The CO, Ted Luce, came up and said 'What's left?' and I remember saying 'Ten men from that platoon and a few from this.' 'Well,' he said, 'Form up, we haven't much time. We are going over. At 05.00 that depleted company went over.'

Lieutenant Colonel Ted Luce, pre-war

The Wiltshire men advanced up the open slope, not dissimilar to the chalk hills of their home county.

> 'After the drop shorts you couldn't blame the men for being a bit jumpy as we advanced straight into corn fields expecting to have great rows of machine guns firing at us. But we got into the enemy position relatively easily and then we started meeting the SS who were well dug in.'

The Battalion's history recounts that:

> '...their objective was the area of the road junction on top of the ridge of Hill 112 but east of the summit top... against dug-in SS, in elaborate deep dugouts in the centre of a web of roofed over crawl trenches leading to weapon pits with Spandaus.'

Without cover from hedges and banks, the SS Grenadiers had resorted to the type of defensive positions that they had used on the open Steppe of the Eastern Front, where they had been fighting little more than a month earlier. However, under cover of a barrage of fire from 8/Middlesex's Vickers machine guns and the tanks of A Squadron 7/RTR, 4/Wilts managed to penetrate the enemy outpost line and the main defences. The Battalion's history continues:

> *'It was a confused soldiers' battle with many individual actions, flushing out SS in dugouts, verifying the "deadness" of corpses, watching for hidden snipers or bypassed Spandau teams or mortar positions. Lieutenant JP Williams was shot by SS as enemy raised their hands in surrender, some of them wearing Red Cross armbands. Corporol Frank, one of the stretcher-bearers with B Coy, tried to succour Lieutenant Williams who died in a few minutes. Frank was attacked by two wounded SS men so he had to shoot them.'*

Captain Robbins experienced some problems as he moved through the enemy position with B Company's headquarters.

> *'Some of the SS let us go over their well-concealed trenches; some of them in one man slit trenches, a sort of cylindrical hole in the ground. Then they would pop up and shoot you from behind or have a go at the reserve company, who were hoping that the front company had done what was necessary. I remember seeing one of our company stretcher-bearers, a very gentle fellow, having an awful time tending an officer. He got very angry as some Germans attacked him while he was doing*

German answer to the American Bazooka – the *Panzerschreck*.

this. He took his Sten gun from around his neck and shot them up.'

Major John Duke, Battery Commander of 224 Battery, 94th Field Regiment, in his White half-track, enjoyed an elevated position above the corn and saw the early stages of the advance.

'We quickly ran into heavy mortar fire and found many wounded men crawling around in the standing corn, and dead German SS anti-tank gunners lying around their guns. Bombardier Nobbs was soon able to report to RHQ on his wireless that we had reached the first objective and Gunner Cox got a German Spandau and opened fire on some enemy infantry who appeared over the Hill. [It was] a tremendous relief to see at last over the hill and to get some shooting on a wide range of targets.'

Major Duke was wounded shortly after reaching the top of the hill by some new arrivals on the battlefield – Tiger tanks.

Panzerkampfwagen VI (Tiger) tanks arrive on the battle scene.

II SS Panzer Corps were fearful that the *Frundsberg's* mounting casualties and the likely loss of their forward positions on Hill 112 would compromise the Corps's entire position north of the Orne. They decided to deploy their decisive weapon, at what they saw as the crucial stage of the battle. It was supreme bad luck for the Wyverns that the delayed Operation JUPITER was launched the day after II SS Panzer Corps's Tiger Battalion arrived at the Normandy front. Twenty-eight of the fifty-six ton Tiger tanks, armed with the dreaded 88mm gun, had arrived by road at the village of St Martin, on their own tracks. This was only two kilometres from the crest of Hill 112 and 4/Wilts at the centre of the British attack. 43rd Wessex Division's deception plans and operational security had clearly been lax.

SS-Mann Heinz Trautman as a junior member of 3rd Platoon, 1st Company 102 Heavy Panzer Battalion, was on guard:

> 'something was on... the MGs were rattling away and the thunder of the artillery rose minute by minute to a howling crescendo. And this "Schützenfest", this firework display, seemed to be only a few kilometres from our resting place.'

Preparing for their first battle together (some were veterans; others were little more than raw recruits) the Tiger crews were found by British artillery shells while they were still preparing to move to their standby positions. SS-*Rottenführer* Willi Fey ordered Trautmann and the crew into the tank:

> 'Gunther Hensel and I were packing all the blankets and coats into the "Africa box" and we were late obeying orders. There was the scream of a shell and I was hit in the leg. I saw Gunther sprawling in a flowerbed, the back of his head torn open. He lay there, curled up as if asleep. Gunther, who had been looking forward to his first operation.'

First Company's Tigers moved to positions that dominated 130 Brigade's advance across the low ground to the east. Meanwhile, Second Company assembled in positions where they could counter-attack onto the open ridges of Hill 112, threatened by 4/Wilts. Eventually the order came to go into action, as the British approached the 10th SS Panzer Division's 'Stop Line'. SS-*Hauptsturmführer* Endemann's Second Company, with its seven operational tanks organized into an HQ and two platoons, advanced into the clouds of smoke that shrouded the slopes of Hill 112, heading up the spur onto the plateau, towards

A knocked out Tiger on Hill 112. This Tiger is a Platoon leader's tank from 2nd Company 102 Heavy Panzer Battalion.

A 6-pounder anti-tank gun and crew in Normandy.

the only visible feature; the isolated group of trees to the south-east of the crest. As the Tigers crossed the ridge, 4/Wilts's anti-tank guns engaged them from the east. The first shots struck with such force that tank 213 was spun round, but Tiger 212 destroyed one of the anti-tank guns before the British gunner could lay the hairs of his sight on a second target. As time passed, a stalemate set in between 4/Wilts and 21 SS Panzer

Grenadier Regiment, despite the intervention of the Tigers who were holding a part of the eastern crestline. On the northern, slope 4/Wilts, supported by the 17-pounder guns of 129 Battery 86/Anti-Tank Regiment RA, maintained a tenuous toehold on the plateau's edge. A hull down Tiger, with only its almost impregnable 80mm thick armoured turret visible above the crestline, pinned down Lieutenant Franz Wallerstine's troop of undergunned 7 RTR Churchills. He sent his troop sergeant, Bill Taylor, back down the hill on foot to summon a tank destroyer to take on the Tiger with its 17-pounder. In charge of the supporting M10s was a pre-war Devon Territorial soldier, Sergeant Cummings. He knew only to well the likely result of an ill considered intervention in the lightly armoured M10!

'I was told by a sergeant from the Tanks that they had a problem for me to sort out. Four Churchills had been knocked out by a Tiger that was hull down a few hundred yards away. So I recced the way forward, decided the range was 400 yards, went back and under cover and gave orders to the driver and gun layer. We went out steadily and the layer spotted it right away. I gave the order to fire and we got the Tiger with the first shot. I don't think it had a chance to see us, as we came right out of cover and fired! We went back but we were later called forward to have a go at some machine-gun nests that were holding up the infantry.'

An M10 repairing tracks before action.

Despite the equalizing effect of the M10's 17-pounder gun, it was lightly armoured and was no match for a Tiger in a sustained open battle. The stalemate continued in this very open part of Hill 112 with the 4/Wilts unable to make headway and the Germans unable to drive them back into the Odon Valley. As he rested in a ditch alongside the road that was his Company's objective, Captain Robbins looked at his watch:

'My God, it feels like teatime but it is still only 8.30 in the morning! It seemed such a long time since dawn. So much was happening in such a short time, with everyone being so excited, people being killed or wounded and many of us killing a German for the first time.'

4/ Somerset LI's attack on Point 112

As the Somerset Territorials lay in their FUP, they contemplated the difficult task that lay ahead. The battalion was to advance across 1000 metres of open ground to their first objective on the Caen to Evrecy road. This was a similar distance to that which 4/Wilts had to cover. However, the shape of the ground was very different. The convex slope on which 4/Wilts had attacked had given them cover for much of their approach from all but the lightly held German outpost line. However, the Roman Road that was 4/Som LI's 'centre line' or axis of advance, made its way up a concave slope. This meant that the attacking troops would be in view of 3/21 Panzer Grenadier Regiment's main positions from the moment they crossed the start line.

The open ground across which the Somersets attacked towards Hill 112.

Forward edge of SS positions in hedgeline

Roman Road

START LINE

Axis of attack

Major John Majendie, commanding Support Company, was in charge of organizing the deployment of the battalion in the FUP, as his mortar and machine-gun platoons had been attached to the rifle companies.

' In the darkness, it must have been about 4 a.m., the battalion moved into its assault positions. We were well drilled in the occupation of FUPs, so it went smoothly. Except the reserve squadron of tanks that we were expecting, failed to turn up.'

Major Majendie had a minor but pressing problem just before H Hour.

'I had a very old pair of school braces, which I was very proud of, and, at a very inconvenient moment, they snapped. I can't remember how I effected running repairs but I do remember that my trousers didn't come down during the attack.'

The attack began in the first light of dawn. Almost immediately enemy fire started to take its toll on the Somersets and their supporting armour. Major Majendie remembers:

'...We came on several deserted German slit trenches with stick grenades laid out beside them and I remember being surprised how very close they were to our starting positions.'

These were the German forward outposts. Despite the creeping bombardment that had helped to keep the defenders' heads down during the initial stages of the attack, casualties were soon on their way back to the Regimental Aid Post. Walking wounded made their own way back, while the more seriously wounded were left where they fell; their presence marked in the waist-high wheat by bayonet and rifle, often with a steel helmet added for good measure. The following tale illustrates the point:

'Edward Trotman, who was the company commander of A Company, was hit fairly early on in the attack by two or three machine-gun bullets. They ricocheted off the silver whisky flask that he had in his breast pocket and wounded him in the arm and leg. He was lying on the ground with his batman looking after him when either a carrier or a tank came up behind them in the corn and his batman only just saved him from being run over. Maj Trotman's main concern was, however, that the medics would not conclude from the strong smell of whisky pouring from the bullet hole in his flask, that he was drunk!'

Casualties to men and armour mounted quickly the closer 4/Somerset LI got to the enemy position. Sergeant Hole of the Somerset's Mortar Platoon, looking up the hillside from the area

4/Somerset LI FUP

Odon Valley

A Spandau gunner's view from the hedge which was the forward defensive position of 3/21 Panzer Grenadiers, (1999).

Spandau gunners await the enemy advance.

of the FUP, described what he saw in the dawn light:

'The whole scene was illuminated by burning carriers and tanks. Flame throwers were in action. The enemy, using Nebelwerfers, was mortaring the advancing troops. Practically every weapon was in use – rifles, grenades, phosphorus, machine guns and tanks – and casualties were extremely heavy.'

SS-*Hauptscharführer* Kurt Level's section of three Mark IV tanks from 5 Company 10 SS Panzer regiment, positioned on Hill 112, exacted a heavy toll on the British armour before being knocked out. They were quickly replaced by the stand-by section under SS *Hauptscharführer* Mathias Borekott. These men, who were later killed, bought time for the remainder of 5 Company's tanks to deploy to the flanks, where they continued to inflict damage on the attackers.

As the Somersets advanced, fighting was at close quarters and Commanding Officer, Lieutenant Colonel Lipscombe (known to one and all in the Somersets as 'Lippy') was fighting between the two forward companies.

Lieutenant Colonel Lipscombe

'The CO was in a Bren gun carrier with his IO [Intelligence Officer] *Gordon Bennet, and at one stage, fairly early in the attack, a German with a hand-held Panzerfaust popped up out of the corn. The CO threw a grenade .*

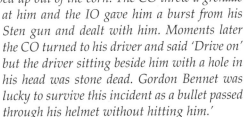

at him and the IO gave him a burst from his Sten gun and dealt with him. Moments later the CO turned to his driver and said 'Drive on' but the driver sitting beside him with a hole in his head was stone dead. Gordon Bennet was lucky to survive this incident as a bullet passed through his helmet without hitting him.'

SS-*Sturmbannfürer* Karl Sattler

The forward edges of the main German defences, held by SS-*Sturmbannführer* Karl Sattler's 3/21 SS Panzer Grenadiers, was sited along the line of a hedged bank, bordering a field immediately north of the road. The Somersets were no longer advancing at walking pace through waist-high corn but were dashing forward from cover to cover. They moved when the fire slackened or when the force of NCOs' and officers' leadership compelled the infantrymen to defy logic and advance. It was inevitably a slow process. 4/Somerset LI had to clear each slit trench individually, while under fire from other mutually supporting trenches. To make matters worse, some enemy positions had been by-passed and came to life after the leading companies had moved on. Private Len Newton of B Company recalled how determinedly the SS panzer grenadiers fought:

> *'Just to the left of the company there was a young German laddie in a slit trench who popped up and started throwing stick grenades at us and several of us shot at him. He was hit. He reappeared again and threw another grenade. He was hit. He reappeared again and so on, until he eventually succumbed. He was a very brave young man!'*

By 09.00 with the Battalion's forward and reserve companies hopelessly intermingled, the number of casualties high and tanks being knocked out all over the hillside, the attack –

> *'...ground to a halt just about on the line of the main road and the Commanding Officer decided that the companies should dig in there and form a firm base. Further attacks were pointless, because by this time companies which were normally the strength of about 100 were down to something like 20 – 30 and platoons which should have been 30 men down in some cases to 4 or 5.'*

This was coincidentally 4/Somerset LI's first objective, tantalizingly close to the crest of the hill at Point 112, which was little more than four hundred metres ahead. But with the 10th Panzer Division's artillery and *Nebelwerfers* of 8th *Werfer* Brigade concentrating their firepower on the Somersets, the distance was immaterial. Worse still, German tanks had intervened again!

7/RTR had been suffering casualties. Thus far, C Squadron had lost Churchills to both *Panzerfausts* and to anti-tank guns in the corn. However, as the infantry were hastily digging in, it was apparent that German panzers were in action around the small woods that crown Hill 112.

The remaining Mark IVs of 5 Panzer Company had moved up to the crest as the Somersets reached the Caen – Evrecy road. The tanks came into action a platoon at a time, as 4/Somerset LI closed with German infantry's main position. This reduced the shock action of the intervention of a mass of armour but, when the feared Allied fighter-bombers were circling above, presenting a small target was imperative.

4/Somerset LI's war diary records a message from B Company on the Battalion's left flank, '09.33. Enemy counter-attacking with tanks and infantry'. Sergeant Morgan, who commanded one of the Somerset's 6-pounder anti-tank guns, had just deployed his gun and has left a description of the action as the first enemy tanks appeared:

10 SS anti-tank gun position in the open fields of Hill 112.

> 'Two anti-tank guns were in a position guarding the flank of the left companies when there was a German counter-attack put in on this front, catching us facing the wrong way. Quickly realizing the situation, we swung the guns around to face the enemy. As a cornfield obscured the view of the guns it was not possible for sights to be laid on the Hun tanks in the normal way. By using an unorthodox method of laying, both of the guns fired through the corn. So successful was this method that three Hun tanks 'brewed up' and the fourth retreated hurriedly, smoke pouring from its turret.'

The war diary records the successful engagements but this was only the beginning for the Somersets. A further counter-attack by another platoon of SS *Hauptsturmführer* Hauser's 5th Panzer Company was similarly costly but their presence confirmed Brigadier Mole's view that Lieutenant Colonel Lipscombe's decision to halt on the line of the road was correct. In a series of increasingly terse exchanges over the radio he convinced Major General Thomas that 4/Somerset LI could achieve little more and, indeed, would be lucky to hold what they had gained so far.

For the remainder of the morning, the afternoon and into the

91

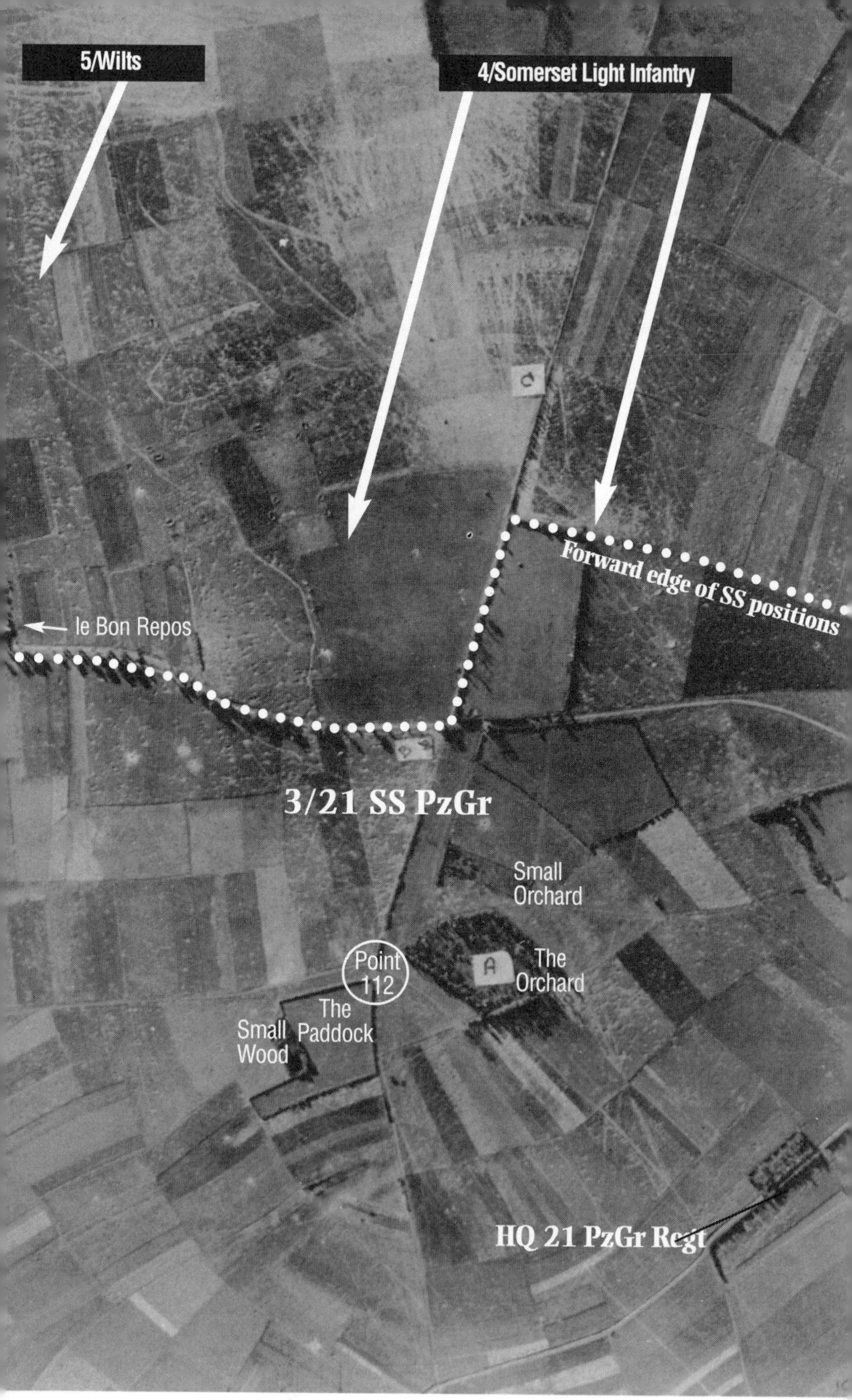

5/Wilts

4/Somerset Light Infantry

Forward edge of SS positions

le Bon Repos

3/21 SS PzGr

Small Orchard

The Orchard

Point 112

The Paddock

Small Wood

HQ 21 PzGr Regt

evening 4/Somerset LI was in the front line holding a piece of ground that 10th SS Panzer Division were under pressure from II SS Panzer Corps to recapture. The Somersets were either under an unremitting fire from artillery and *Nebelwerfers* or being counter-attacked. The defence of Hill 112 was declared II SS Panzer Corps's *Schwerpunkt* or point of main effort. In support of this aim the Germans applied all available resources to stop the advance of 4/Somerset LI and prevent them crossing the 'stop line' and gaining the top of Hill 112. The *Nebelwerfer* fire had certainly played its part but most telling had been the volume of small arms fire. An officer of the Somersets, Lieutenant Sydney Jarry, has given his considered opinion as a front line platoon commander with ten months almost continuous experience of fighting the Germans:

'It took me a few weeks to realize what their little game was. When we attacked a German position the problem, though a simple one, was very difficult to overcome. Vastly superior infantry firepower, both small arms and anti-tank, was their trump card. A German infantry platoon could produce about five times our own fire power. There was just no way through the curtain of fire from the MG42s. Sometimes, by stealth, we were able to bypass it; otherwise artillery or armoured support was necessary – often both. But due to their excellent anti-tank guns, the 75mm and the 88, the use of armour could prove costly.'

Relatively early in their Division's first set-piece battle it was apparent to commanders at all levels in the 43rd Wessex, that they had many lessons to learn. Tragically, in war lessons are always learnt at the cost of dead and wounded men. Max Hastings in his book *OVERLORD* described Operation JUPITER as 'a battle of shattering intensity even by the standards of Normandy' and the extreme circumstances exposed the lack of experience in the Wessex Division.

5/Wilts

5/Wilts were to attack from the small village of Baron on the banks of the Odon in 'Death Valley'. The Battalion had taken and held the village since 29 June 1944 and from this position they had been able to mount numerous recce patrols of no man's land and their Operation

le Bon Repos

5/Wilts

B Coy

Phase 1

D Coy

Phase 2

C Coy

Hill 112

Caen-Evrecy road

The road from Hill 112 down to Bon Repos was the objective of C Company 5/Wilts. Having reached this point they got into difficulties on the open slopes.

JUPITER objectives. They were to attack strongly held positions on the north-west slopes of Hill 112 that lay between 4/Somerset LI and the hamlet of le Bon Repos. Unlike the rest of the Division, 5/Wilts were to attack enemy positions that lay downhill from their start-line in Baron. Their mission was to clear positions astride the Caen – Evrecy road and then to form a defensive flank, facing south-west in order to protect the remainder of 129 Brigade on the top of Hill 112.

In common with the day's other initial advances, the leading companies, B on the right and D on the left, reached their objectives under the cover of a bombardment, which included smoke to cover their right flank. The Wiltshires were surprised how well the enemy outposts were dug-in, but the power of the British artillery, directed against the enemy position had quickly cleared the stunned SS Panzer Grenadiers. Sergeant Reg Romain, commanding a 6-pounder anti-tank gun was in support:

> 'We formed up behind D Company. The enemy spotted us and started to shell and mortar our start line. The gun would have been useless in all that fire, so we looked for a bit of cover and jumped into an old trench only to find a dead German in the bottom. The smell was awful and I jumped back out again. I shall never forget watching our men go forward into the hell of tank fire, mortar, machine gun, shells. You name it, Jerry was slinging it at us.'

Once on the objective the companies dug-in north of the road, spurred on by an increasing volume of accurate shell and mortar fire. The next phase of the Battalion's attack was for C Company and the Carrier Platoon to attack through the leading companies, in order to destroy the enemy positions in depth along the crest of the hill, before falling back. This was a far more difficult objective to take. The accompanying 17-pounders of 86/Anti-Tank Regiment were of great assistance, some giving close support to the infantry, others standing back engaging targets as they presented themselves. Again, seemingly against the odds, the Wiltshires were successful but, in a very exposed position, they were quickly pinned down by heavy fire and were unable to move. Captain John McMath recorded in the regimental history:

'C Company advanced up Hill 112 and despite mortar, shelling and small arms gained the top astride the Caen – Esquay road but were pinned down by dug in tanks and machine guns firing from Esquay. CSM Smith in a Bren gun carrier bringing up ammo, saw a tank shooting its way along the road towards the prostrate company, grabbed a PIAT, ran through the cornfield, fired it from the hip and knocked out the tank, for which he received a merited MM. There were well dug-in and well defended enemy artillery OPs on the hill constructed many months before.'

So firmly pinned down were C Company that they remained stuck in a forward position all day. A Brigade level plan had to

An 11th Armoured Division Sherman knocked out during Operation EPSOM is used as a German artillery OP.

Prisoners from 8 *Werfer* Brigade taken 10 July 1944. *Wehrmacht* and SS prisoners were separated.

be organized to extricate them at about 17.00 hours. This operation included Corps level artillery support from the medium guns of the AGRAs and a feint attack by 4/Somerset LI to the Battalion's left.

46 Highland Brigade's attack on Louvigny

15th Scottish Division had detached 46 Brigade, along with its divisional artillery, to come under Major General Thomas's command for Operation JUPITER. The Brigade's task (see map p 58):

> '...was to give left flank protection to 43rd Division's attack and clear the apex formed by the Odon and the Orne east of Eterville. There, towards Bretteville-sur-Odon, the 46th Brigade was to make contact with 8th Canadian Brigade.'

One battalion, 9/Cameronians, was to take up defensive postions at Eterville, as we have already seen, and the other two were to attack in an easterly direction astride the River Odon. The advance began at 09.45 hours. On the north bank, the 2/Glasgow Highlanders had their start-line at Verson and on the south the 7/Seaforths advanced from Trette Poux.

The **Glasgow Highlanders'** advance punched into thin air to the north of the Odon. The capture of Carpiquet Airfield and the fall of Caen had led SS Panzer Corps to withdraw the *Hitler Jugend* to positions with the 1st SS, south of the river. To have remained north of the Odon they would have been in an exposed position inviting destruction, sandwiched between the advancing British and Canadians. So hurried had their departure been that there were none of the usual nasty surprises

such as mines and booby traps, habitually left
behind by the SS, for the advancing British. By
midday, the Glasgow Highlanders had reached
the forward positions of 8 Canadian Brigade south
of Bretville-sur-Odon. The historian of 15th Scottish
tells of an incident caused by dust:

> 'At 2 p.m. they handed over to the Canadians
> and withdrew through Verson into reserve in the woods
> on the southern bank near Rocrenil. Unfortunately
> the dust of their withdrawal was seen by the enemy,
> who still held the commanding spur that runs north-
> eastwards from Eterville to Louvugny. "No dust, no
> shells." The Glasgow Highlanders had a number of
> casualties from mortar-fire.'

At this point in the battle, a reserve battalion
would have been most welcome, as 130
Brigade's situation on the left flank of Operation
JUPITER was still precarious. However, the
Glasgow Highlanders, were still moving
with difficulty into reserve behind the
Seaforths and were consequently not available
to support either 129 or 130 Brigades at Hill 112 or
Maltot at a crucial point in the battle.

To the south of the Odon, 46 Highland Brigade's third
battalion, 7/Seaforth Highlanders, along with B Squadron
7/RTR had more of a battle. They found themselves fighting
along 1st SS Panzer Division's battle outpost line, which was
dominated by the enemy's main positions on the Eterville –
Louvigny ridge. The plan was to advance on a company
frontage, in four bounds, with each company taking its turn to
lead. The first three bounds went well but the fourth, by D
Company, found the enemy very active in the area of le Mesnil.
If 4/Dorsets and 9/RTR had not been successful in and around
Eterville and taken much of the *Leibstandarte*'s immediate
attention, the task of clearing the valley would have been far
more difficult. The Seaforth's attack was complicated by the fact
that it was through hedgerows, woods, farms and orchards.
Consequently, in close Bocage type country, their progress was
much slower than that of 2/Glasgow Highlanders on the north
bank of the Odon and it was only 'After hard fighting they
reached their objective, le Mensil, about 7 p.m.'. Here they

6 Troop, B Squadron, 7/RTR supported 46 Brigade's attack, 10 July 1944.

eventually made contact with the advancing Canadians who had been advancing from Carpiquet towards Louvigny.

The Seaforth's regimental history recounts the tale of a German operator, speaking very good English, joining the Battalion's Mortar Platoon radio net:

1st SS
Leibstandarte
Panzer Division

> *'During the action, a voice came on the Mortar Officer's set – "You think you can shoot, see how German mortars shoot", and a stonk landed all around him. "Are you still there? Good shooting, yes?" Back went the answer: "Bloody awful, is this better?" and stonked four likely spots. No more was heard.'*

An SS Panzer Grenadier Company HQ beneath a knocked out tank.

CHAPTER FOUR

OPERATION JUPITER
Attack on Maltot village and Cornwall Wood

130 Brigade's attack on Maltot

While 129 Brigade's advance on to Hill 112 was checked on the German 'stop line', 130 Brigade, who had taken the German forward positions at Chateau de Fontaine and Eterville, launched 7/Hampshires, into the depths of the enemy's defences. Their objective was Maltot and the woods on the ridge to the south of the village. The plan was that with Maltot taken, 4 Armoured Brigade would then advance to the River Orne crossings and the open 'tank country' beyond. Success of this advance beyond Chateau de Fontaine and Eterville was predicated on 129 Brigade taking the dominating Hill 112 feature and denying its fire positions to the enemy. This had not happened, despite some heroic efforts against the well prepared 21 SS Panzer Grenadiers and the Tigers of 102/SS Heavy Panzer Battalion.

Heinz Harmel, in his command vehicle, directs operations in the Maltot area.

By 06.00 hours, 7/Hampshires were waiting to occupy their FUP south of Fontaine Etoupefour, which had already been used by both 4 and 5/Dorsets. On receipt of a report at 08.16 hours that objectives had been reached along the Caen to Evrecy road, 7/Hampshires, with A Squadron 9/RTR, advanced between the Dorset battalions towards Maltot. 'This...' as the Regimental Historian records: '...entailed a long advance down the forward or enemy slope of the ridge through tall ripe corn with but little cover'.

Joining the advance were two companies of 5/Dorsets, who advanced on 7/Hampshires' right flank. Artillery Forward Observation Officers (FOOs) in carriers, half-tracks and in Observation Post variants of the Churchill, mounting dummy guns, moved with the advancing infantry. The OC of 220 Battery, Major Penrose, travelled with the Hampshires' commanding officer, Lieutenant Colonel DWG Ray, and one of the FOOs, Captain Paul Cash advanced with the leading companies. They were on hand to accurately adjust fire onto the village of Maltot and opportunity targets. However, intelligence was that 'the village was lightly held if at all' and, consequently, there was to be no mind numbing barrage to subdue the Germans. At 08.35 hours 9/RTR recorded that they ran into trouble. The adjutant, Captain John Hodges, described what happened:

> 'The tanks reached the orchards surrounding the village and the infantry entered. At this stage, everything seemed to go wrong. The tanks were caught in a murderous cross-fire from beyond the river on their left and from the woods and reverse slope of Hill 112, the latter being the objective of 7/RTR who failed to take it.'

What had gone wrong? The Hampshires, who were supported by 5/Dorsets and A Squadron 9/RTR, had penetrated deep into the enemy positions. The cross fire from anti-tank weapons from the left flank of the advance was from the remnants of 1st and 12th SS Panzer Divisions, while the shot and shell from the area of Hill 112 and Maltot came mainly from 1st Company, 102/SS Heavy Panzer Battalion, who had moved into battle positions from St Martin. One platoon remained on the dominating reverse slope ridge of Hill 112, while the second platoon of four tanks, under command of SS *Oberscharführer* Baral, rushed down to Maltot, arriving at almost exactly the

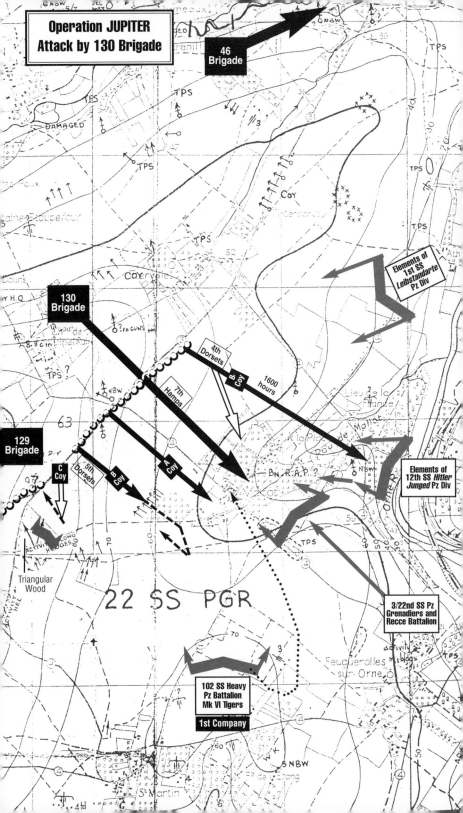

Operation JUPITER
Attack by 130 Brigade

46 Brigade

130 Brigade

129 Brigade

4th Dorsets

B Coy

1600 hours

7th Hamps

5th Dorsets

C Coy

B Coy

A Coy

BN R.A.P. ?

Triangular Wood

22 SS PGR

Elements of 1st SS *Leibstandarte* Pz Div

Elements of 12th SS *Hitler Junged* Pz Div

3/22nd SS Pz Grenadiers and Recce Battalion

102 SS Heavy Pz Battalion Mk VI Tigers

1st Company

Mk VII Churchill. It was heavily armoured but seriously under-gunned and stood little chance against anti-tank guns and panzers. This Churchill is in position on Hill 112 today and acts as a memorial to the British soldiers who fought and died their in the summer of 1944.

same time as the Hampshires. The Tigers pushed through the narrow streets of Maltot and reached the northern side of the village. SS *Rottenführer* Willi Fey commanded the leading tank:

'We reached the edge of the village. Wasting no time, we pushed through the hedges. There in front of us were four Sherman tanks [Churchills?]. *Panzer halt! On the left hand, tank 200 metres. Fire at will! Two rounds finished off the one on the left, the one on the right suffered a similar fate and our platoon commander pushed forward to knock out a third. The fourth sought safety by rushing back along the road! It was a great boost to our young panzer crew.'*

All German accounts describe these tanks as Shermans but at this stage of the battle, only Churchills were involved. Probably, the similar profile of the accompanying M10 Tank Destroyer confused them. Recognition of British armour was not the

SS-*Rottenführer* Willi Fey

A Tiger of a German Heavy Tank Battalion west of Caen.

forte of a newly formed unit, in action in the west for the first
time. Whatever the source of the error, what is certain is that
7/RTR and the M10s were fighting for their own lives. In
consequence, they were in no position to lend the kind of help
to the infantry that they had given so effectively at Chateau de
Fontaine, Eterville and on Hill 112.

Despite the presence of the Tigers and lack of barrage, by
09.15 hours, 7/Hampshire had occupied Maltot and signalled
this to Headquarters 130 Brigade by wireless. However, 'In
actual fact, they had merely superimposed themselves on top of
a very strongly held enemy defended locality.' This criticism of
7/Hampshires by Brigadier Essame in the divisional history
forgets that the Division, during five years of training, had
adopted these tactics. The Wyvern's tactical doctrine was to
push through a village bypassing enemy strong points but at the
same time breaking up the cohesion of the enemy's defence.
Once through the leading companies, they were to establish
defensive positions in order to prevent the Germans reinforcing
or counter-attacking into the village. Meanwhile, the following
companies were to clear the houses, buildings and hedgerows
in detail. As a brigade commander in the Wessex Division,
Brigadier Essame should have remembered this. In the case of
Eterville these tactics had worked, albeit more slowly than
predicted, but at Maltot conditions were very different. Firstly,

SS-*Rottenführer* Willi Fey in the turret of Tiger 134.

this was not a frontline position but one in the heart of the enemy defences. Secondly, Maltot was surrounded on three sides by enemy armour and anti-tank guns in positions to the rear of Hill 112, overlooking the village. Thirdly, the presence of Tigers in significant strength unexpectedly swung the balance of forces in the Germans' favour.

On the right flank of 7/Hampshires' advance on Maltot, 5/Dorsets were in action. A and B Companies had objectives in the area of a triangular orchard to the west of the village. B Company secured its objective and was attempting to dig in on the open ground to the south of the orchard, when it found itself the Tigers' immediate target. Driven back to the cover of the fruit trees, B Company left their dead and wounded as a testament to the hopelessness of its task while Hill 112 remained occupied by the enemy. 5/Dorsets' memorial stands on the open slopes of the Hill looking down on Chateau de Fontaine and Maltot; a view that the SS panzers were using to their advantage. A Company was more fortunate; it had veered to the left of its objective and was eventually located nearer the outskirts of the village. To help 9/RTR who were suffering heavily from the fire of Hill 112, C Company 5/Dorsets was brought up from reserve to advance and clear a small triangular wood. This was in fact a small field hedged by trees occupied by infantry of 21 Panzer Grenadiers, along with three tanks, possibly Tigers. The enemy infantry withdrew as the British artillery and mortar fire lifted and the leading platoons charged. However, the Dorsets were to find that bayonets were of little use against the panzers spitting machine-gun fire from mutually supporting positions. The Company withdrew back towards Chateau de Fontaine. Still in forward positions, A and B Companies were ordered to attempt to assist 7/Hampshires in Maltot but were under such pressure themselves that it was all they could do to hold their positions. They remained all day in hastily dug, but continually improved, slit trenches to the west of Maltot, subjected to both German and British artillery fire.

Once in Maltot, 7/Hampshires' leading companies attempted to push on through to the ridgeline to the south. Major Gordon Viner commanding A Company recalls that,

'I was relieved to capture the first hedgerow and get a foothold in the village but to advance further proved negative as the village was heavily defended by numerous Tiger tanks and well-

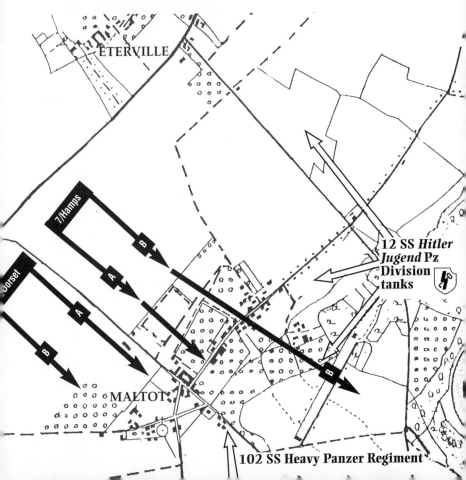

trained SS troops, both well concealed and dug-in.'

B Company, on the left, was more successful and, under a growing weight of fire, advanced some three hundred metres south-east towards the wooded banks of the River Orne. Here it ran into the remnants of the *Hitler Jugend*. Few soldiers of B Company survived the encounter and those that did were nearly all wounded and found themselves prisoners of war. Nineteen year old Private Davies of B Company was one of

Nobby Norman and his crew in front of their Churchill tank.

the wounded who was eventually taken prisoner. He has written that:

> 'Major Tompkins yelled for us to charge.... We chased the remaining enemy out of the gardens killing a few on the way and rushed through the alleys to the road and on to the other side. The village looked deserted and the houses undamaged, ground floor windows were boarded up but glass was intact in some of the higher windows... On the south side of the village in the rear gardens we were met by a Mark IV tank [not the Churchill they had been expecting] which blasted us with heavy MG and explosive shells. Major Tompkins yelled for us to charge the woods about fifty yards away to our half left. For about an hour – though it could have been much longer – we played a cat and mouse game with the Germans, each side taking pot shots at anything that moved. At some time in the afternoon I was hit by shrapnel from two hand grenades. ...It was evening when the Germans finally rushed us.'

At 09.55 hours, 7/Hampshires' war diary records that forward elements, 400 metres south of Maltot, were attempting to dig in

Sergeant Nobby Norman and three of his crew being questioned by Harmel after their capture near Maltot. The shock of being knocked out and captured is evident on their faces. See action on page 104.

but counter-attacks were making it '...imperative to withdraw – Tigers and infantry attacking from south-east and the south-west.' Meanwhile, among the houses, Battalion Headquarters, C and D Companies attempted to clear the village in detail. They found to their cost that it was prepared for defence and held in strength by 22 SS Panzer Grenadier's Engineer and Reconnaissance Companies. The enemy had sheltered in the cellars dug deep into the limestone and had emerged behind 7/Hampshires' leading companies. Private Jim Jones vividly remembers fighting amongst the houses:

'The windows and doors of some of the houses were boarded up. We soon realized that these were the defended ones. As we passed on through, we fired into them and posted grenades where we could. We thought that we were taking a lightly defended village as promised by our HQ. But they [the Germans] came to life once we had passed.'

The Hampshires may have driven off, or at least subdued the defenders for a period, but at 10.35 hours their war diary records that 'nine of our tanks KO. German inf sp by Tigers

The business end of a dug-in German 88mm anti-tank gun.

infiltrating back into the village. Being heavily mortared'. However, their problems had really begun somewhat earlier. Following close behind the rifle companies and the Commanding Officer's party were the 'soft skin vehicles' of Main Battalion Headquarters with the Battalion's only truly reliable radio sets. Parked alongside a building in Maltot's main street they were soon destroyed, having just confirmed to 130 Brigade that they were in control of the village. Left with only man-pack radios to pass messages back, the Hampshires were effectively out of touch with their brigade headquarters, as the rough treatment entailed in fighting in villages took its toll on the sensitive, valve technology radios. In addition, the radio operators were soon too busy fighting for their lives to want to fight for communications. At 10.15 hours, against mounting opposition, the Commanding Officer was wounded while attempting to organize his battalion in strong points at the centre of Maltot. Patched up, he was back in action and commanding his Battalion's defence at the village crossroads, but little more than fifteen minutes later he was wounded again. A soldier nearby saw 'A number of Hampshires tied white handkerchiefs to their rifles... Lieutenant Colonel Ray stood up and shouted, "I will shoot any man myself who waves a white flag" and was fatally wounded.' The RMO was killed while trying to treat his commanding officer for a second time. Things went from bad to worse, with the second in command also being wounded. Major Phillips, of C Company, assumed command of the Battalion.

Back at Headquarters 130 Brigade, as far as the staff were concerned, 7/Hampshires were safely occupying Maltot. Despite increasingly desperate requests for artillery fire made by Major Penrose and 220 Battery's observation officers, they were not shaken from the view that all was well. To be fair, the entire divisional effort was focussed on 129 Brigade's foundering attempts to take key positions on the crest of Hill 112. To that end, all of 112/Regiment's guns, not involved in maintaining the smoke screen on the left flank, were firing on Hill 112. The key to the battle was possession of 112. If it was not taken, the advance on the low ground by 4 Armoured Brigade would probably fail. It would seem that the fact that 7/Hampshires were already well into the low ground was, without reports from their battalion headquarters, ignored.

On the German side, SS-*Brigadeführer* Heinz Harmel, commander of the 10th SS Panzer Division, quoted in one of the Frundsberg's histories, summarized the situation at this stage in the battle:

'Whilst our divisional and corps artillery, together with 8th Werfer Brigade, brought down a heavy curtain of fire to prevent the British developing their attack on the top of Hill 112, the [3rd] armoured battalion of the 22nd Panzer Grenadier Regiment and the 10th SS Reconnaissance Battalion were moved forward to counter-attack at Maltot with the support of Tiger tanks from 102 SS Heavy Battalion.'

Heinz Harmel as an SS-*Oberführer*.

The Hampshires' war diary describes what happened to this counter-attack:

'It was not until the enemy were actually entering the battalion positions that the call for [artillery] fire was finally granted. A very accurate barrage was laid just forward of the fields ...This undoubtedly saved the position.'

The village of Feuguerolles-sur-Orne, and Harmel in his command-post half-track organizes the counter-attack against 7/Hamshires in Maltot.

By 11.56, 9/RTR were reporting that 'the situation is in the balance at Maltot'. Both 7/Hampshire and A Squadron were under severe pressure from the counter-attacks. In fact, the armour and infantry were fighting separate battles for survival, unable to support each other. The Churchills and their accompanying M10s were fighting a losing battle with mounting casualties, against the German armour, who were able to 'jockey' from position to position on the ridge above the Maltot area. This gave both British armour and infantry the impression that they were up against almost overwhelming numbers of enemy tanks. They weren't! However, the Germans were using Tigers that had vastly superior firepower shooting from excellent positions. The Adjutant of 9/RTR described the results of the battle:

> 'At this stage about three-quarters of A Squadron had lost their tanks and were trying to get back one way or another. The Padre and our own ambulances made repeated attempts to get forward to the squadron and succeeded in picking up about twelve men but the position was impossible.'

Bombardier Douglas Lakey MM, a part of an FOO's party has told of the last stages of the fighting in Maltot in very personal detail:

> 'My Bren carrier was then set on fire by an incendiary, the Sergeant signaller was still in the vehicle relaying instructions to the Corps artillery. At one time we ordered "fire as fast as you

can", having previously given them our location – something went wrong and the medium shells all fell on our position. Meanwhile, I had taken up a position behind my vehicle and was using a machine gun to fend off advancing infantry. A platoon of German infantry could be seen a couple of hundred yards away advancing on

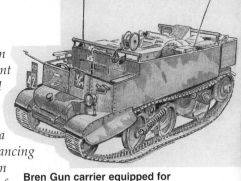

Bren Gun carrier equipped for signalling.

our position – the carrier was on fire and ammo was getting low... I waited a few seconds until the German platoon had to pass a gap in the hedge and then gave them the full blast of machine-gun fire – they faltered and I shouted to my trapped colleague to get out [of the carrier].

'Suddenly I heard the roar of a Panzer a few hundred yards to our rear and looked round saw this huge monster with gun equally huge pointing towards us. Diving flat on the ground just in time to evade an armour piercing shell which the Panzer fired. The shell passed literally a few inches above my posterior – the fragments of steel from the hole it made in my vehicle showered my backside and it was like a pin cushion with all the needles pushed in... I ran into the orchard and was lucky to see a dug-out made by the Germans and it had a wood cover. I ran into this and there found three others, all British.

'The Germans soon overran this area and were riddling these dug-outs with machine-gun fire. We soon realized this was likely to be our end and we shook hands and prayed – there's nothing

A knocked out Bren Gun carrier and 6-pounder destroyed south of Maltot.

Ruins of Maltot village after the fighting.

like this to make a man pray. We heard the rattle of Army boots running over the top of us – the spasmodic burst of gunfire as they raked the dugouts. Our thoughts raced through our heads – what would my folks at home be doing – how would they react to the formal notice of killed in action. One of the soldiers in this dug-out was having a puff at his last and only cigarette – in a state of nerves he would have a puff and then pass it to his mates to do likewise. Myself, I was resigned to be either killed or captured. I was not afraid, just filled with regret that all the future things I had planned and hoped for were now just vanishing.'

The OP carrier of Captain Paul Cash. It was destroyed by a Tiger tank at Maltot. Bombardier Douglas Lakey MM, is on the left.

Stalemate

By 13.00 hours, a stalemate had set in across the front. 10th SS Panzer Division with elements of I SS Panzer Corps had contained the British advance on their 'stop line' but the Germans were still dangerously exposed. It had taken virtually all their combat power to achieve this and reinforcements from 9th SS Panzer Division were still some distance away. The war diary of Panzer Group West recorded the following 'Sitrep' at 14.00 hours:

> 'In the course of the morning the enemy succeeded in capturing Eterville and Maltot. But all assaults on the dominating feature, Hill 112, were repulsed.'

It is clear from German reports of 10 July 1944, that they fully appreciated Montgomery's strategic aims. However, so compelling was the threat of a British breakout to the east, that they could do little but respond to the attacks on Hill 112, just as Montgomery had intended. On the other side of the hill the 43rd Wessex had few reserves available to continue the attack, other than 4 Armoured Brigade. In a particularly terse exchange, Brigadier, later Field Marshal, Lord Carver came under pressure to join the battle. However, he felt that the conditions to launch his lightly armoured Sherman tanks had not been met.

> 'The Churchills of a squadron of 9 RTR supporting the final phase of the attack being almost all knocked out by anti-tank fire from this wood [the Orchard on the crest of Hill 112], which the infantry had not cleared. Having confirmed this myself when I took my tactical headquarters forward... I said I would not order my leading regiment over the crest towards the River Orne until the wood had been cleared of enemy as agreed... [Major General] GI Thomas came on the [radio] set himself and said

The western end of Maltot with the dominating ridge beyond used by German tanks.

1st Company
102 Heavy Panzer
Regiment

that his information was that all objectives had been secured, and that I must start my forward thrust. I said I was on the spot and his infantry brigadiers were not, and that if he did not believe me he could come and see for himself. This, not surprisingly, did not please him. He insisted that I should order my tanks to advance over the crest. I said that if I did, I expected that the leading regiment would suffer 75 per cent casualties... and not reach their objectives. He asked me which regiment I proposed to send. I told him it was the Greys [Scotland's only Regular Army cavalry regiment]. *'Couldn't you send a less well-known regiment?' he replied, at which I blew up. Finally, he accepted my arguments, but relations between us... were permanently soured.'*

With hindsight, it could be argued that 4 Armoured Brigade's intervention at this stage could have been decisive in breaking the stalemate before the arrival of 9th SS Panzer Division. The cost would, however, almost certainly have been very high. The fate of the more heavily armoured Churchills would indicate that Brigadier Carver's estimate of his leading regiment's casualties would probably have been correct. History would also have had to compare tank casualties for Operation JUPITER with those suffered, little over a week later in 'the death ride of the British armoured divisions' during Operation GOODWOOD.

At 15.00 hours, a commanders' conference assembled in the tower of the Fontaine Etoupefour church. From here, Major General Thomas and his brigadiers could see that the situation around Chateau de Fontaine and Eterville was far from quiet and Hill 112 had obviously not been taken. This conference decided three things. Firstly, that 4/Dorsets who were now in reserve between Chateau de Fontaine and Eterville should immediately move to the support of 7/Hampshires in Maltot. Secondly, that, despite the understandable reluctance of Brigadier Carver to attack, elements of 4 Armoured Brigade were to be brought south of the Odon in order to secure gains against German counter-attacks. This was because there was a very real concern that the Germans were proving to be far more numerous than anticipated and that a powerful counter-attack could drive the division back across its start line and beyond. Elements of three SS panzer divisions had been identified and the *Hohenstaufen* was known to have been relieved in the line by

The church at Fontaine Etoupefour. During the fighting it was used as the Anchor O.P. site for 122 Field Regiment RA and subsequently by Major General Thomas to review the progress of the battle. See pages 56/57 for view from church tower.

277th Infantry Division. The third, and most important, decision was that 5/DCLI in their assembly area north of the Odon should dismount from their Kangaroo armoured personnel carriers and move by foot to the bottom of Hill 112. They were the Division's only other uncommitted battalion and were to renew 129 Brigade's attack on the high ground. Captain Pat Spencer Moore, Major General Thomas's ADC, summed up his general's dilemma:

'It was clear to the GOC that only a completely fresh attack on Hill 112 could stabilize the battle – perhaps even win it – or perhaps incur even more shattering losses? It was a gambler's throw by Thomas. The only problem was that he was gambling with the lives of hundreds of his well-trained but completely green young soldiers. It must have been a terrible decision... .'

Meanwhile, at 15.00 hours, a counter-attack by 20 SS Panzer Grenadiers Regiment confirmed the urgency of the need to support 130 Brigade at Maltot and at Eterville. Artillery fire slowed both attacks but finally Typhoons, diving down on the enemy vehicles moving in the open, halted the German advance. Once again the effect of the feared jabos spitting

115

Ruined house at Maltot.

cannon fire and rockets had been proved. However, against concealed targets and single fast moving vehicles they were far less effective, hence their inability to be of much help to 129 Brigade on top of Hill 112.

4/Dorsets

Having being relieved in Eterville, 4/Dorsets had barely two hours to reorganize after their heavy casualties and reload with ammunition before orders came to 'move now' to support 7/Hampshires at Maltot. There was little time to spend planning, 4/Dorsets' companies were simply allocated quadrants of Maltot to reinforce, marry up with Churchills of C Squadron 7/RTR and advance southwards. As little was known except that the Hampshires were still in the village, there was to be no fire support from artillery. Company Sergeant Major Laurie Symes recalls the battalion's mood:

> 'My company – D – formed up for the attack on the reverse slope in front of Chateau Fontaine waiting for the off. I was in the company Bren gun carrier which was loaded with the company's reserve ammo. Neither, myself or my driver gave a thought at the time what would have happened to that lot, if we had been hit by an 88. The whole company had their tails up for this attack and were eager to go. I looked up the slope to see

116

Major Eastwood, our company CO up front with his walking stick and whistle. When the time came, off we went through the standing corn.'

The Dorset's move at 16.00 hours coincided with the final act of 7/Hampshires' defence of Maltot. As 4/Dorsets approached the village, they met the remnants of the Hampshires withdrawing from the ruins. Once the repeated German counter-attacks had gained a foothold in Maltot the Germans could not be effectively engaged by artillery and air support, for fear of hitting 7/Hampshires, who were eventually overwhelmed and were now withdrawing.

In a recording made in a captured German trench, somewhere on the ridge between Eterville and Maltot, the BBC news reporter, Chester Wilmot, recorded these words while looking down on the northern outskirts of the village:

'By now that wood was enveloped in smoke – not the black smoke of hostile mortars but white smoke laid by our guns as a screen for our infantry who were now being forced to withdraw. We could see them moving back through the waist-high corn and, out of the smoke behind them, came angry flashes as the German tanks fired from Maltot. But even as the infantry were driven back another battalion was moving forward to relieve them, supported by Churchill tanks firing tracer over the heads of the advancing men. They moved right past our hedge out across the corn. The Germans evidently saw them coming, for away from our right flank machine guns opened up and then the Nebelwerfers... .'

Two days after the battle, the *Wyvern News*, the divisional daily newsheet, printed amongst news of the raising of travel restrictions to the West Country and improvements to Service pay, a comment on Wilmot's report.

'People at home last night on the 9.00 p.m. News heard a broadcast of the fierce fighting around MALTOT in which our units were engaged. The recording made within 500 yards of the most forward positions, was most vivid. One recording designed to give an impression of the din of battle gave the sound of 'Moaning Minnie' mortar shells arriving and bursting. The announcer was blown into a ditch and left the recording machine running. The striking words at the end of the report were "and now the infantry, who have been in the centre of all that, are up and moving forward again through the shattered cornfields.'

Sergeant Stevens's troop several months after the battle.

During the advance, Corporal Chris Portway records the horror of 4/Dorsets' second encounter of the day with their own airforce's ordnance.

> *'A squadron of our own rocket firing Typhoons dropped out of the sun in twos and threes with the noise of an express train: the field seemed to rise up in flames; there was a great noise of rending metal. Rooted to the spot, we gazed upwards as another plane dived; we saw the wings shudder as the rockets were released. Explosions tore at the tortured earth. We hung on with our bare hands clutching the soil. My comrade at my side became a messy gore of rags. In front of me was the company dispatch-rider with no legs. A man came running out of the dust and smoke, total bewilderment on his face.'*

This terrible description of a tragic 'own goal', only too common in war, uses many of the same words and phrases as Germans do when describing Jabo attacks.

Sergeant Geoff Cleal, still with Advanced Battalion Headquarters remembers, equally bitterly, that:

> *'During the advance to Maltot we were pinned down in standing corn, some of which was burning. We were trapped rabbits at harvest time. Every time we made the slightest movement, we were greeted with a burst of machine-gun fire. It*

was frightening to hear the bullets hitting the corn above my head.'

Sergeant Jim Stevens, with his troop's three remaining M10s, was supporting the Churchills of 9/RTR:

'E Troop pushed on towards Maltot when the second M10 was put out of action by an airburst over that bloody open turret, wounding the gun crew and putting it out of action. The third M10 was hit by an 88 in the front, killing the driver and wireless operator. Slivers of steel from the inside of the hull, wounding the troop commander in the neck and the No 1 sergeant in the back. They escaped through the hatch in the bottom of the M10, as German machine gunners were firing at the turret. They both made it back to the RAP.'

By 16.45 hours most of 4/Dorsets had reached Maltot and were attempting to consolidate in defensive positions. But once again they had superimposed themselves on German positions and confused fighting resulted. Corporal Chris Portway, with the leading companies, describes the action at the edge of the village:

'We were in an empty tank pit sheltering from the mortar fire and sorting ourselves to continue, when we saw a coal scuttle

A knocked out M10 of E Troop showing the open turret.

H.P. or B.H.P.	Petrol Tank Capacity	Average miles per gallon	Bore or Stroke	Magneto		
				Make	Type	Regt. No.
S.P.235224 M10 E.1.	Elevating & traversing			gear	U.S. 7	
S.P.235229 M10 E.2.	Bogie wheels	& Hull		perforated		
S.P.237830 M10 E.3.	Burnt out		10.7.44		88 m	
S.P.235165 M10 E.4.	Burnt out		10.7.44		Mortar	
L.5434270	3 Ton (1)					
L.5284476	3 Ton (2)					
T125616	CRUSADER	RECCE				
F07951	A.O.P.	BREN GUN CARRIER Burnt Out	15.9.44		88mm Best	
"	A.O.P.					
S572298	JEEP	Vehicle accident				

Sergeant Jim Steven's notebook. The first four entries record the fate of his four vehicles during Operation JUPITER.

helmeted head peer over the rim. But he was too slow and we got him with a single shot before he could stick grenade us... We burst out of the pit firing in all directions and headed for the nearest house. We smashed our way in, which I have always regretted as it occurred to me at the time that I wouldn't have liked it if it were my house. Clearing each house, we moved on until in one we were sorting out our remaining ammunition, when we heard movement upstairs. We listened and aimed shots through the ceiling above where we thought the Jerry was. We missed and he sent a shower of grenades down the stairs and holes in the floor. Fortunately no one was seriously wounded and we eventually got him.'

The divisional history records that:

'Lieutenant Colonel H.E. Cowie, the CO, arrived at the HQ of 7/Hampshires on the outskirts of the village just behind his leading companies. Too late [he] learnt that what remained of 7/Hampshire were being withdrawn. Meanwhile his two leading companies, expecting to take over from the Hampshires advanced straight into the enemy position and were surrounded. ...enemy tanks worked round to the rear of the remainder of the battalion, which lay out in the fields, exposed to fire from every direction. The position had become desperate!'

Size of Tyres				Width of Track	Wheel Base	Remarks
Rear		Front				
Size	Pressure	Size	Pressure			*Area*
10·7·	44		O.K.	13·7·44	*taen.*	*Maltot,-112*
10·7·	44	OK.	*Handed over to*		*taen*	*7 Yk. Sgt Tucker maltot 112*
					"	*Maltot 112*
					"	*Eterville 112*
	?		*Written off*	U.S.		*Feel Grainbasg fak.*
1·8·44			*Handed over.*			*Best.*
2·9·44 -			*written off*			

A Company had followed the same course as one of the
Hampshires' companies and advanced so far to the south-east,
that they were lost to a man. Over the next three hours in Maltot,
4/Dorsets' platoons and sections fought their own cat and
mouse battles with the SS Panzer Grenadiers. Overall control of
the battle was beyond any one person and the riflemen
progressively lost contact with their battalion, company and
even platoon headquarters. A troop of towed 17-pounders, from
130 Battery, who accompanied the Dorsets, deployed to form an
anti-tank screen around the south of the village.

> 'They were quickly overrun in a German infantry counter-
> attack and after expending all their small arms ammunition,
> removed the breech blocks of the guns and retreated to the
> infantry slits [trenches] losing half the troop in the process.'

The Battalion's Mortar Platoon were, however, able to provide a
greater amount of support. Private Frank Porter recalls:

> 'We were firing all day from the Odon Valley but I don't
> know what at. We only got the direction, elevation and charge
> that we were to use. We didn't have the asbestos gloves that we
> were supposed to have, so we used wetted sandbags to move the
> barrels that were so hot that the paint had burnt off. The mortars
> got so hot that there was a danger of the bombs exploding before
> they left the barrel.'

Outside the village, it was C Squadron 9/RTR's turn to fight an

SS-*Oberführer* Heinz Harmel, commander 10th *Frundsberg* SS Panzer Division, liaises from an armoured personnel carrier with an SS-*Hauptsturmführer* of the *Leibstandarte* Division during the British attack on Louvigny.

unequal battle with the superior tanks of I and II SS Panzer Corps. The enemy armour that had worked its way around the village was engaging the Churchills shortly after 17.00 hours. Sergeant Trevor Greenwood's memoirs describe what happened:

'And then I noticed one of our tanks on fire. What was happening? There were no signs of enemy on the hill, and our infantry were in the woods and village. It seemed like a counter-attack in force, judging by Major Holden's further appeal. He had somehow contacted the infantry commander. And then the Major's voice... he wanted help ...smoke. He got smoke... all of us poured it out as fast as we could. In a matter of seconds, our former peaceful hill crest [half way between Maltot and Eterville] was pretty well littered with burning vehicles – and smoke. I noticed one or two nearby vehicles moving away, but where to? Soon I couldn't see a thing but smoke, but gave the driver orders to advance: better to go anywhere than stay and be shot up. Eventually I found my way back to lower ground away from the danger zone ...but I was still hazy about the situation.

All the same, I felt convinced that something pretty bad had happened.'

Sergeant Jim Stevens's troop was still in action.

'The fourth M10, realizing that the Churchills that they were supporting had nearly all been destroyed, took up a hull down position and invited some infantry who were being slaughtered, to come on board for protection. They replied "Not bloody likely you'll not get us in that steel coffin." I think that says it all!'

At 20.30 hours, three hours after they entered the village, the remnants of 4/Dorsets dug in on the northern outskirts of Maltot and were given permission to exfiltrate back towards Chateau de Fontaine and Eterville. Sergeant Caines was with those who withdrew:

'The CO, Battalion Headquarters, parts of B, C and D Companies, and the Carrier Platoon withdrew under extremely accurate support from 112th Field Regiment. We passed back through 7th Somersets and took up a position in the area of Horseshoe Wood. During the withdrawal I went back with R.S.M. Drew to help bring in a private soldier who had a foot blown off, and who up till then had been hopping along on his rifle; he remained quite conscious until we got him to an M.O.; only then did he pass out.'

Meanwhile the remains of C Squadron had already withdrawn and joined the remainder of 9/RTR to rally in original FUP before moving back to join A Echelon north of the Odon.

Only a minority of the Dorsets got the message to withdraw. Corporal Portway and others from his platoon were among those who were not told to move back.

'...the rattle of the gunfire had gradually died away, leaving only a solitary rifle shot here and there. It was a strange silence, an eerie sense of solitude. There were five of us in a ditch. We knew what had happened. The battalion had gone. We hadn't heard the order. There was only one thing to do. Wait for darkness and then try to get back... Then the artillery opened up again. This time it was different: a scream of shells and the village became a hell on earth. We were on the wrong end of our own artillery bombardment... We pressed down deeply in the ditch, no longer completely in control of our own actions, the fearful noise annihilating our senses... I kept my eye fixed on a dandelion close to my head. It was my anchor in this

Armageddon. Silence again; a silence as loud as was the noise...
Then German voices – German voices. Would they pass by?
Then I saw blood trickling down the shoulder of my jacket. The
man next to me was dead. Guttural voices and exclamations.
Three German soldiers stood above us. We lifted our hands in the
air.'

In driving both the Hampshires and the Dorsets out of Maltot, the Germans had eliminated a salient deep into their defences north of the Orne. They followed up their success, under the cover of gathering darkness, with counter-attacks by elements of 10th SS and 1st (*Leibstandarte*) SS Panzer Division. They managed to penetrate 9/Cameronians' defences in Eterville from the left flank. A night of deadly fighting ensued before they were finally ejected.

Of those Dorsets who fought in Eterville and Maltot only five officers, including the CO, and less than eighty other ranks gathered in the area of Horseshoe Wood. This figure does not include the ten percent 'Left Out of Battle' for just this circumstance; to act as a core around which to rebuild the battalion. CSM Symes, who collected the remains of D Company has summed the situation up with typical understated West Country reserve: 'A lot of brave men came out of Maltot and a lot were left behind'. 7/Hampshires also suffered cruelly. They lost eighteen officers and two hundred and eight other ranks. The Territorial heart of the brigade, built up over years of pre-war service and five years of home defence and training, was ripped out in a single day's battle. In common with many other divisions, the character of the units under command of 43rd Wessex Division changed forever. A very different division fought on all the way to Bremen.

5/DCLI's Attack on Hill 112

The attack of 5/DCLI on Hill 112 late on 10 July 1944, was the final offensive throw of Major General Thomas's Operation JUPITER. It was without doubt one of the most tragic acts of self-sacrifice in the entire North West European Campaign. By early evening it was clear that a break through to the Orne was not possible. The leading elements of 9th SS Panzer Division were beginning to arrive and the Tigers of 102/SS Heavy Panzer Battalion had ensured that no further progress had been made at Maltot. On Hill 112, stalemate had persisted since late morning and it is hard to escape the bitter conclusion that a prize had to be taken for the sake of vanity. That prize was to be the possession of Point 112. The observation posts looking south from the Hill did, however, offer the possibility of successfully renewing the battle for the Orne crossings. Was this potential prize worth the sacrifice? Commander 4 Armoured Brigade had earlier refused to commit his Sherman tanks to battle because of the likely casualties but Brigadier Essame, Commander 214 Brigade, records a different view:

> '*By about 3 p.m. it was clear to him* [Major General Thomas] *that only a completely fresh attack on Hill 112 could stabilize the battle. Two of the three battalions of 214 Brigade had already been committed at Chateau de Fontaine. There remained only one battalion available which might still turn the tide. This was 5 D.C.L.I., now snatching what rest it could on the outskirts of Fontaine-Etoupefour. Neither Major-General Thomas nor the commanders of 129 and 214 Brigades, who were with him when he made this decision, were under any illusions as to the necessity of the grim task now to be given to the D.C.L.I. Neither had their commanding officer.*'

The reader will draw his or her own conclusions as to the merits of the two views.

Lieutenant Colonel Dick James had taken command of 5/DCLI just fourteen days earlier, when his predecessor was killed at Cheux during Operation EPSOM. At twenty-six years of age, a pre-war Territorial soldier and Somerset solicitor, his charismatic personality made an instant impact on his new battalion. At 17.00 hours Dick James and OC A Squadron 7/RTR were given orders at Headquarters 214 Brigade in the village of Fontaine-Etoupefour. Two hours later, he gathered his company commanders and commanders of supporting arms in 4/Somerset LI's forward positions. Here he gave his orders, from a spot where commanders could see the 400 metres of open ground that they had to cross to reach their objective; a large orchard and paddock on the crest of Point 112. If 5/DCLI, assembled for

Lieutenant Colonel Dick James

orders, needed any illustration of the seriousness of the situation, an attack by Tigers and Panzer Grenadiers was broken up by artillery fire on the lower slopes of Hill 112, while they were being briefed. In the limited time available Colonel James's plan was perforce simple; a heavy bombardment followed by an advance directly on to the objective, supported by A Squadron 7/RTR. In the failing light of dusk, arrangements were far from the standards of perfection achieved in the Battalion's five years of training. However, an intimate knowledge of what was required of them made up for the lack of time. 5/DCLI, in common with the rest of the Wyvern infantry, was a very good battalion.

To save confusion, at this point in the narrative it is necessary to define names for the three 'woods' that were the scene of 5/DCLI's action. Confusion between 'woods' has also been the source of much post-war disagreement as to who actually held Hill 112. Two of the 'woods' were in fact orchards surrounded by banks covered in trees and bushes that, from the infantryman's view, looked like woods. The one nearest to the British lines will be referred to as 'Small Orchard', while the large orchard on Point 112 will be known as 'the Orchard'. The name 'Small Wood' will be used for the trees on the German side of the hill that surrounded a small overgrown quarry. The

The Orchard

Site of small orchard

two orchards were clearly marked on the 1:25,000 planning map but the Small Wood was partly obscured by over printing. However, on the smaller scale 1:50,000 map, used by commanders in the battle, only the Orchard is marked – in the wrong place! It had been moved 200 metres to the south-east, so no wonder there were so many friendly artillery fire incidents!

At H Hour, 20.30 hours, 5/DCLI, who had formed up in dead ground behind 4/Somerset LI's positions, attacked across the frontline along the Caen to Evrecy road. Their objectives were the orchards and the crest of Hill 112, little more than 400 metres forward of the Somersets' trenches. 'Two assault companies 'C' Company right, 'B' Company left, would provide the initial thrust, with 'A' and 'D' in close support.' 5/DCLI attacked, supported by all the guns available including the Bofors guns of 110/Anti Aircraft Regiment who had precious few *Luftwaffe* planes to worry about. The stream of rapid fire from the Bofors made up for the lack of tank support for the leading companies, as A Squadron 7/RTR was late arriving at the FUP. The tanks joined the rear companies and were quickly in action in support of A Company, who had to intervene and suppress enemy fire from the Orchard that had caught B Company in the open. Private Jack Jones of 8/Middlesex [divisional MG Battalion] was a part of Major Kenyon's Mortar Fire Control party, who moved up onto Hill 112 on the left flank of the Cornwalls with B Company.

Point 112   Paddock   Small Wood

Roman Road

> *'We came under heavy fire and casualties were mounting and the attack stopped. We put our carrier in an excavation where a German tank had been hull down. Major Kenyon said, 'I'll find what's holding us up'. When he came back he redirected the guns and mortars and soon we moved forward again.'*

Following up with D Company was a soldier, Private Gordon Mucklow, who had been transferred to the DCLI from the Warwickshire Regiment:

> *'We reached half-way to the [Small] orchard, pausing in a dip across the field. Stick grenades were being thrown at us from the edge of the orchard. We must have been only just in reach. The officer with us shouted, 'throw them back', which we did. We were elated to see we could do it with some success, as the time delay fuses were longer than ours. The Jerries then ran from their positions.'*

Under heavy fire and with their own grenades falling about them, the SS Panzer Grenadiers retreated from the Small Orchard and enabled the now depleted B Company to occupy the southern hedgerow of the main Orchard. B Company, with only forty men, was to hold this dangerously exposed position,

A British 17-pounder of 59 Anti-Tank Regiment and its Quad tractor knocked out on the plateau of Hill 112 near the orchard.

receiving the constant attention of enemy fire. Following behind, A and D Companies reached the ditch that divided the Orchard and started to dig in. Following the fleeing Germans was too great a temptation for one of the Battalion's five Canloan officers, Lieutenant Carmolli, who led his platoon of D Company down the hill in pursuit. He and most of his men were killed, with the rest being taken prisoner. Meanwhile, on the right, C Company had fared well against little opposition but had veered off to the south-west where some of them appear to have headed through a hedge and across a paddock towards the Small Wood. Little is known of their fate. However, some members of C Company joined A and D Companies in the defence of the Orchard. While reorganizing Private John Mitchell, D Company signaller, with his company commander:

'...moved forward and found ourselves on a long track going south, we were now a small group. Suddenly a tank came out of cover, we raced to the bank to get into the wood again, with machine-gun bullets everywhere. The bank surrounding the wood was steep with little grip even for army boots and I was carrying an 18 Set. I got up that bank and you know it was sheer fear that helped me! We made it to a large crater, my Company Commander Major John Fry, two sergeants and my signals mate. I found that my battery was flat but I had passed a dead signaller as we made for the crater and I went back to find him. It was Lionel Blanchard, the first signaller that we lost, with his radio set still on his back. He had been shot through the transmitter into his back. I removed the battery – thank God, there was still some life left in it. ...Major Fry gave me a map reference. I encoded it and asked for smoke cover from the artillery. In minutes smoke shells fell almost on top of us. We thanked God for our wonderful gunners!'

Under cover of the smoke, the companies sorted themselves out into some semblance of order.

At 21.00 hours the report that 'British tanks have taken Hill 112' started to make its way up the German chain of command from 3/21 Panzer Grenadiers. On the ground SS-*Rottenführer* Zimlitz, ejected from his shelter by B Company 5/DCLI, recalls that:

'When the Tommies got into the Wood of the Half Trees [the German name for the Orchard] *we moved to our last line of retreat. It was a dry stone wall overgrown with bushes, about a*

hundred metres further down the slope. It gave good cover and a good field of fire. Behind that ditch, the slope ran downhill for a thousand metres without a scrap of cover. We always said that we would have to hold that ditch or die in the attempt. Tommy never got that far.'

As 21 SS Panzer Grenadiers reported the loss of Hill 112 they were at the same time preparing a counter-attack. Meanwhile, in the Orchard, 5/DCLI were busy preparing to defend the banks and hedges. The historian of the DCLI describes the mood:

'Behind the rifle companies and on the flanks were the anti-tank platoon with a troop of artillery 17-pounders. In support, they found positions from which to meet the inevitable counter-attack. It was not long in coming and in the failing light, supported by a heavy bombardment, German infantry and tanks stretched every nerve to regain the wood and Point. 112.'

The remaining Tigers of 102/Heavy Panzer Battalion and two companies of SS infantry made the counter-attack. SS-*Obersturmführer* Schroif and his platoon of Tigers were waiting at the southern foot of the Hill:

Tiger concealed on the edge of a wood.

'It was almost dark when the order came. On the right, I could see the Tigers of No 1 Company already moving on to the slope. My objective was the Kastenwäldchen [another German name for the Orchard]. We got to within about three hundred metres of it. I halted the Company and opened fire. I pushed forward on the left into a hollow in the ground. We couldn't have been more than a hundred metres away. We fired with machine guns and sent high explosive into the tree tops. Machine-gun fire rattled on the armour and we could see the muzzle flashes of the anti-tank guns.'

Major Roberts describes what happened as the German infantry came through the Orchard's southern hedge:

'We had no difficulty in repulsing the infantry, the fire discipline being first class and both companies giving Boche absolute hell. It was grand to hear the section commanders shouting out their orders 'Hold your fire, chaps, until you see the bastards' eyes!'

With the SS infantry checked by the combined fire of 5/DCLI and the artillery, the Tigers were unable to press home their attack. Fearing to close within range of the Cornishmens' PIATs they withdrew. The account given in the DCLI history continues:

'The attack was repulsed, largely because of the remarkably good fire-discipline of the battalion by means of which a heavy and accurate fire was brought to bear on the attackers. Major Roberts records that along the tree lined ditch he could hear, between bursting mortar shells, the section commanders firmly ordering their sections to hold their fire until they could be sure of their mark. In consequence the fire of the defence was highly effective and when what remained of the enemy had withdrawn, the defenders began to dig as vigorously as they could, much impeded by roots, for they knew they must expect an early repetition of what they had just experienced.'

During and after this attack the vulnerability of towed anti-tank guns became apparent to the DCLI. The shields of the Battalion's 6-pounders and the 59/Regiment RA's 17-pounders gave protection against small arms fire and shell splinters from the front. However, the gunners, who had to be in at least a kneeling position to serve their guns, were totally exposed to the flank and rear. Even when dug-in and sheltering in the large

131

British infantry digging in during Operation JUPITER.

open topped gun pit, the gun crew were vulnerable to air burst shells. 5/DCLI, as was common among infantry in Normandy, also suffered heavily as a result of large splinters of wood being blown down by shells exploding in the trees above them.

Throughout the action the number of anti-tank guns available to 5/DCLI was steadily reduced and reliance on the short range (and not very accurate or reliable) PIAT became greater.

The second counter-attack came around midnight. This time the Germans closed in on the Orchard, as it became apparent to the Panzer Grenadiers that B Company had abandoned the forward hedge. The enemy tanks, believing that they had overrun the DCLI's position, roamed around the battalion area. Private John Mitchell describes one incident:

John Mitchell

'*My mate and I were digging in, in the second last hedgerow from the crest. We both cried out in dismay as the hedge came down on top of us, a Panther most likely, was pivoted on the bank and*

132

we were underneath, with the tracks either side of us. The large gun on the tank fired, it was deafening, so much so we hardly heard the shell that hit the underbelly of the tank inches from us. It was a 'Piat', fired by one of our lads at close range. The Panther backed off the bank as it was possibly damaged.'

Counter-attacks came and went. With fewer anti-tank guns still in action, the SS panzers made regular forays around the Hill. Between attacks, Sergeant Frank Grigg, Signal Platoon Line Sergeant, was at 5/DCLI's Advanced Battalion Headquarters in 4/Som LI's frontline.

'Hardly noticing that the shelling has eased off (too busy digging) the signal officer appears "I want a line party to take a line to the wood" he says. Most of the signallers were already deployed with their companies and those handy were nearly all NCOs. Standing with one foot up on a dead cow he says, "Now chaps, here's medals on your chest". Sergeant Gould, a Londoner, mutters "I don't want any bloody medals on my chest" but this is ignored or drowned out by shelling. Where is our fifteen cwt truck with all the gear? It must be at the rear. Three of us take a drum of cable each, phone, pliers, tape and earth pin. Off we all go into the darkness. "This way" says the signal officer as he dashes ahead. I can't go that fast as I pay out the cable stumbling along the rough ground. Nearly the end of the drum. Suddenly the Signal officer turns directly to the right "God! Where's this dammed wood." The drum gives a wrench. "Wait" I hiss "we have to make a joint." Kneeling down Corporal Jack Foster and I struggle to make a reef knot in the cable, twist tape round. Suddenly a Verey Light lights up the whole scene. We freeze, motionless! [they were hoping to be mistaken for part of the landscape] London humour now comes from Sergeant Gould "Whoever saw a drum of cable growing out of a tree!" Blackness as the light goes out. We go on. Damn this noisy spindle on the drum; bound to give us away. God! End of second drum ...Another Verey Light. This time from a tank coming around the end of the wood. Friend or foe? We don't know. It starts firing tracer bullets at us. "Get down Sergeant Grigg" shouts the signals officer "They're after you!" He's right behind me so I say "Well he must be after you too sir!" But the Verey Light gave us a glimpse of the hedge and Colonel James just inside. The signals officer and Jack Foster jumps over with the telephone and I clamber in with the cable. Hastily we

Dividing Hedge

N

The Orchard today. The fruit trees were not replanted after the war. Still evident is the ditch and hedge that divided the area and gave 5/DCLI some cover.

connect the telephone; "Hello, Rear HQ" says a voice. Good we're through, thank God! Suddenly we're aware of the tank to our left, which has now moved closer. It stops, out jumps a crew member, "Kamerad, Kamerad" he shouts. "Shoot him", yells somebody but signallers have no weapons! "Here's a Verey pistol", says someone. The signals officer takes the pistol and shoots the poor sod. He reels like a Catherine wheel on fire! And the tank roared off.'

Pressure was mounting as 5/DCLI's strength was gradually reduced by the counter-attacks. There was artillery fire but very little from *Nebelwerfers*. Presumably, being of light construction and located in the forward battle area, they had mostly become casualties to the British artillery. The Mortar Fire Controllers of the Wyvern's machine-gun and mortar battalion (8/Middlesex) however, now occupied the Orchard and not 8 *Werfer* Brigade. In a deteriorating situation, Major Fry of 5/DCLI, not knowing where the commanding officer was, had a difficult decision to take. Jack Jones recalls:

'We were in a ditch just inside the wood about ten to fifteen yards from the eastern corner. The noise of the artillery shells and mortar bombs was deafening. Occasional Verey lights went up and we were bringing fire down on the southern hedgerow. This cacophony went on for ages, then about 03.00 hours two men came along the trench. "FOO!" "Yes." "I am the senior officer of the DCLI and I would like you to report back to [Brigade] Tac HQ, "SITUATION CRITICAL. PERMISSION TO WITHDRAW". Major Kenyon replied "I can't take that message back as a verbal message, you'll have to put it in writing and sign it." This was done in the bottom of the ditch, covered by groundsheets with the light of a map-reading torch. We mounted our carrier and rolled quietly forward down the hill and after a minute or two Sergeant Bob Tighe reached up and*

Jack Jones's night drive into enemy lines

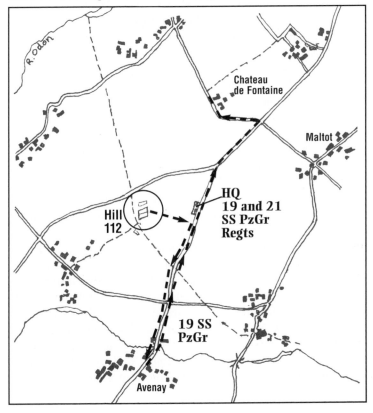

135

pulled both of my radio aerials down. "What's up Bob?" I asked but looking up in the dark I saw the black and white outline of the German cross on a tank that we were passing in front of! Just as we were going under the tank's barrel, a flare went up 200 – 300 yards away. "Foot down Phillips. Get a move on it!" In the pitch black, we belted across the open country.

'After several hundred yards, the carrier dropped a foot or so onto a road and kit shot all over the road. Major Kenyon shouted, "Never mind the kit. Turn right and get moving." I said to Bob, "He's gone the wrong way. He's going behind the Hill!" After a pause Bob replied "He knows what he is doing". About half a mile further along the road, we passed infantry marching on both sides of the road and the occasional vehicle. In front of us, we could see a crossroads with a building on fire. Major Kenyon said that "there shouldn't be a cross-roads and buildings here!" I replied, "I think its Avenay sir". We parked up between two non burning buildings. "Phillips," said Major Kenyon, "get the Bren and shoot anyone who comes through the gap." A couple of minutes later he reappeared and said "Get back in the carrier, all these chaps are Germans!" We started off back up the road and soon caught up with the column of infantry and vehicles, so we joined them! Several times Major Kenyon got off the carrier and went to look at the signposts. We passed a copse where there were lots off vehicles parked up [TAC HQs of 21 and 19 Panzer Grenadiers]. Soon we realized that we were through the infantry and on our own. We made it back to our own lines near Chateau de Fontaine ...We reached 214 Brigade TAC HQ and delivered our message at 05.30 hours.'

The night went on, with 5/DCLI subjected to repeated bombardment and counter-attacks. Their strength steadily ebbed away as wounded were taken to the rear but the dead lay where they fell. Lieutenant Colonel James's leadership and coolness in action were exemplary and did much to ensure that his battalion held its position when many other lesser units would have melted back to the safety of the Odon Valley. Major Roberts, one of the surviving company commanders said:

'The CO was magnificent. He set an outstanding example to everyone by his personal courage, endurance and irrepressible spirit. The position we were in would have taxed the most seasoned troops, and we were still rather green. But for him, I don't know what might have happened.'

The Return of 9th SS Panzer Division

By early July, the Germans had been forced to keep their most mobile and potent forces holding ground rather than being available to counter-attack and seize the initiative from the British. However, with the arrival of 277th Infantry Division from the Pas de Calais, 9th *Hohenstaufen* SS Panzer Division was released, from positions to the west of Hill 112, into reserve. The relief had taken three nights to complete. The SS soldiers, who had been in action since they arrived in Normandy at the end of June 1944, were in urgent need of time to rest, refit and to repair their vehicles. They moved into hides strung out along the wooded valley of the River Orne as far as Thury Harcourt and west to Villers Bocage and beyond. The much-needed rest enabled the 9/SS Repair Battalion to bring the Division's armoured vehicle strength up to seventy-five tanks and assault guns fit for combat. Most importantly, this total included forty-three Panthers of 1/9 SS Panzer Regiment. Overall, on the morning of 10 July 1944, the *Hohenstaufen*'s armoured vehicle strength was just over fifty-five percent of its theoretical establishment. The field workshops had plenty more vehicles that, given time and spares, they were able to fix and so help to maintain the Division's combat effectiveness over the coming days, despite heavy losses. As the units were refitted, they returned to reserve positions from where they could reinforce both II SS Panzer Corps and XLVII Panzer Corps. Elements of 19th SS Panzer Grenadier Regiment were deployed well to the west, behind the boundary between 277th and 276th Infantry Divisions and two battalions of 20th SS Panzer Grenadier Regiment were in close support behind the *Frundsberg*. Their presence was unknown to the British planners and their timely intervention, along with some of the Panthers of 1/9 SS Panzer Regiment, was central to the stopping of 130 Brigade. It must also be concluded that many of the Tigers reported by 7/Hampshires and 4/Dorsets were, especially in the late afternoon, Panther tanks.

On the morning of 10 July 1944, as the scale of the attack and threat of a break-through became apparent, Headquarters Panzer Group West gave authority for 9th SS Panzer Division to return to II SS Panzer Corps command. They were to concentrate in order to mount counter-attacks in support of the hard-pressed *Frundsberg* who were struggling to hold the British. 20th SS Panzer Grenadier Regiment was in action relatively quickly but, previously having been badly hit by British artillery and fighter bombers when counter-attacking the EPSOM Corridor, moving the remainder of the Division back to Hill 112 was bound to be slow. A few vital vehicles could dash from cover to cover but, for the majority, the fifteen mile road move could only be completed in darkness, once the dreaded Allied 'Jabos' were safely back at their bases.

As the *Hohenstaufen* prepared to move, SS-*Standartenführer* Sylvester Stadler took command of the Division. A much decorated and highly experienced soldier, Stadler moved from 4

SS Panzer Grenadier Regiment (*Der Führer*) of the *Das Reich* Division, who had been fighting the Americans to the west. At a crucial point in the battle, a highly perceptive officer of the highest quality took command of the force that was tasked to restore the situation on the Odon front.

With dusk falling, at 22.00 hours, the *Hohenstaufen*'s vehicles, lined up in hides, fully prepared for battle, took to the road. By 23.45 hours 2/9 SS Panzer Artillery Regiment, reported 'ready for action'. However, by 23.59 hours the *Hohenstaufen*'s commander, SS-*Standartenführer* Sylvester Stadler, was reporting that 19th SS Panzer Grenadier's columns had become snarled up with the *Frundsberg*'s and 277th Infantry Division's resupply traffic coming in the opposite direction. With

SS-Standartenführer Sylvester Stadler. Photograph was taken when he was an *Obersturmbannführer.*

no room to pass in the country lanes, 19th SS Panzer Grenadiers were marching the last seven kilometres to the battlefield on foot, as seen by Private Jack Jones during his adventure behind enemy lines! None the less, Stadler, having recced the area, briefed SS *Brigadeführer* Harmel, commander of 10th SS Panzer Division over the radio. 'Bollert's mission, with Hagenlocher, is to take the eastern flank of Hill 112 [1/9 SS Panzer Regiment and 1/19 SS Panzer Grenadiers]'. Orders were later given to the *Hohenstaufen* to take over the responsibility for the attacks towards Eterville and Chateau de Fontaine. The 10th SS Panzer Division had been fought to a standstill in its attempts to contain the Wessex Division's attacks. The 9th SS had arrived just in time.

After midnight, the Germans felt that the task of recapturing Hill 112 was not going to be easy and they were fearful that the longer the DCLI were in the Orchard, the more they would be reinforced. The words of SS-*Mann* Zemlitz, one of the few survivors of his company, illustrate the Germans' concerns:

'One of our mortar sections, firing at the greatest possible elevation into the small wood, gave it everything, but the

The German self-propelled 105mm guns, called the _Wespe_ (Wasp).

Engländer had occupied it in strength.'

Because of the Germans' concern, the first two companies, 5th and 16th (Engineers), of 19 SS Panzer Grenadier Regiment, were placed under command of 21 SS Panzer Grenadiers when they arrived to the south of Hill 112 at 01.20 hours. At 01.40 hours, 1/9 SS Panzer Division Artillery Regiment also reported 'Ready to open fire', with the sixteen 105mm guns of their two self-propelled batteries. However, unable to take short cuts across country, their third (towed) battery with eight 150mm medium guns was still stuck in the traffic jam behind the lines. They did not come fully into action until almost first light. 19th SS Panzer Grenadiers continued to be fed into counter-attacks, piecemeal, as they arrived, until, fearful of a renewed attack from Hill 112, II SS Panzer Corps ordered them into defensive positions to contain a British attack. By 03.00 hours 2/19 SS Panzer Grenadiers were digging in on the southern slope of Hill 112.

With 2nd Battalion in blocking positions along the line of the road, a thousand metres from the top of the hill, 19th SS Panzer Grenadiers launched a series of counter-attacks starting at 04.35 hours. From the south-east, came 3/19 SS and the divisional assault gun battalion and from the south-west, the 1/19 and 9 SS Panzer Battalion. The divisional war diary, however, records that all was not well with the troops regrouping for the attack:

'Hargenlocher (19 SS Pz Gr), south of Maltot, reports that the tanks had not arrived as predicted.' In fact, his company of Panthers would not arrive until dawn. Because of the delays in the Germans' rear area, Number 2 Company of 102/SS Heavy Panzer Battalion replaced the Panthers and attacked with 19th SS Panzer Grenadiers. Their axis of advance followed a lane that ran up the hill from the small village of Esquay. *SS-Mann* Trautmann, a radio operator in one of the Tigers describes the attack:

> 'Shells were exploding on the hull and turret; they were breaking off branches in the treetops! Our panzer grenadiers couldn't even raise their heads. Many brave comrades were left dead on the slopes.'

Willi Fey described the British artillery during the counter attacks:

> 'Down came a barrier of defensive fire such as we Eastern Fronters had never known; the Russians never had as many guns as this, and they did not use them in this way; and then came the thick smoke screen. Our attack folded up at the foot of the hill, before we even got on to the slopes.'

Eventually one of the attacks reached the Small Wood when the Tigers drove blindly through the British artillery fire. The SS Panzer Grenadiers caught up once the British artillery observer covering the approach had been killed or driven off. There

19 SS Panzer Grenadiers attacking Hill 112 up the southern slope. The black smudge top right is an airburst over the orchard on Hill 112.

A battery of 25-pounders in action in Normandy.

followed a short sharp fight with the remains of C Company 5/DCLI. This was the 'lost company' who had been out of touch with its Headquarters since the previous evening. Soon signals were going up the German chain of command to the effect that 'the Kastenwäldchen had been taken!' However, unfamiliar with Hill 112's geography, 19 SS had in fact only captured the Small Wood on the southern crest, not the Orchard, which was still stubbornly held by 5/DCLI. But by first light, 3/19 SS followed by the 1/19 SS had secured positions on the southern

Hill 112 from the south looking up the Roman Road. This slope was littered with the dead and wounded of 9th and 10th SS Panzer Divisions.

Small wood

Point 112

Orchard below crest of hill

1/19 SS
PzGr

3/19 SS
PzGr

Roman Road

From the position of 19 SS-Panzer Grenadiers' position. Clouds of smoke wreath the crest of Hill 112 while the SS prepare for their next attack.

edge of the plateau, on a line through Small Wood and the drystone wall that earlier sheltered 21 SS Panzer Grenadiers. They prepared to attack again and again, if necessary. The Germans had so far failed to completely retake Hill 112 but they had stabilized the situation with a ring of steel that would be difficult to penetrate.

The Defence of Eterville – Night 10 / 11 July 1944

Meanwhile, on 43rd Wessex Division's left flank the situation in Eterville had been deteriorating. 9/Cameronians had taken over the defence around midday on 10 July 1944. A and B Companies were in forward defensive positions to the right and left respectively. C Company was in the centre and D Company was in reserve ready to link up with 7/Seaforths. They completed digging in during the afternoon, all the while under mortar and artillery fire. However, following the withdrawal of the Dorsets from Maltot and the breaking up of several counter-attacks by the guns of 3rd AGRA, the Germans managed to work their way into Eterville. SS Grenadiers now resorted to

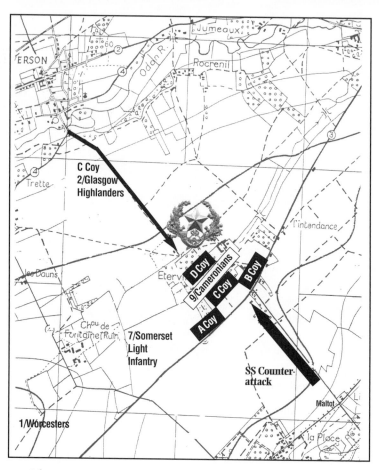

stealth and found a covered approach through an orchard and into a gap between A and B Companies on the perimeter of the village.

'Soon after dark the enemy, about eighty strong, counter attacked "C" Coy. and secured a footing in the right forward platoon position, and then established themselves in an area which cut off "D" Coy. All communication with this Coy. was lost and every attempt to regain touch resulted in casualties. ...The details of the fighting are obscure, but 'D' Coy. HQ ...were never seen again, and were presumed killed. The whole Battalion manned their alarm posts throughout the night, but at 3 a.m. on the 11th the enemy withdrew.'

Having penetrated the Cameronians' positions the panzer grenadiers had run amok in the centre and rear of the Battalion area and at one time, the Battalion's Forward Headquarters had been in danger of capture. The Commanding Officer had a miraculous escape when a mortar bomb exploded only just above his helmet and knocked him unconscious. The Second in Command and three company commanders were wounded. The situation was serious and Brigade Headquarters sent C Company, 2/Glasgow Highlanders to help fill gaps in the defences around the village perimeter. Ordered forward just after first light, C Company took up positions in the orchard to block the enemy's covered route into Eterville:

> 'They were almost immediately counter-attacked in strength by German infantry supported by two or three tanks. This led to a spirited defensive action by "C" Coy., who used their weapons including PIAT guns, with deadly effect. For a short time a party of enemy got a footing in the orchard, but Corporal Losimer led his section in a bayonet charge and soon dislodged them. In this action ammunition supplies were nearly all exhausted, the Company reserve ammunition arriving only just in time. When the enemy finally withdrew over 100 German dead were counted.'

In addition to the 4/Dorsets' casualties in taking the village, the defence of Eterville had cost 9/Cameronians, one officer and twelve other ranks killed and thirty-nine missing, but they also lost a total of 149 wounded. This was the third occasion that this Battalion had suffered this scale of casualties in less than a month. It was no wonder that Montgomery looked over his shoulder in horror at the rapidly dwindling pool of infantry replacements.

The Cameronians were not the only ones having a difficult night on the low ground to the left of Hill 112. Outside the village of Eterville, 20 SS Panzer Grenadiers, having regrouped and reorganized after retaking Maltot, were preparing to follow up their success. At 04.00 hours, timed to coincide with one of 19 SS's attacks on the DCLI, 1/20 SS (left) and 2/20 SS Panzer Grenadiers (right) attacked with the aim of containing 130 Brigade. By 04.35 they were between Maltot and Eterville and were reported as 'progressing well beyond Maltot'. This is not surprising, as the Wyverns had remained on the reverse slope, roughly along the line of the Caen to Evrecy road. While it was still dark one 'Point group reached the Caen – Hill 112 road and found it unoccupied. Patrols sent forward to recce enemy position. Engaged from the right [direction of Eterville] by MG fire.' The same report also describes that the

> 'Patrol penetrated the position between sleeping sentries and captured a machine gun before alerting the enemy who wounded one grenadier. Having alerted the enemy, the patrol withdrew under cover of the captured machine-gun's fire, our MG 42 having had a very rare stoppage. A second patrol penetrated the enemy line without being seen and reached a mortar position. They sabotaged the enemy position and snatched some binoculars from sleeping soldiers.'

It would appear that 20th SS Panzer Grenadiers, despite their minor patrol successes against 130 Brigade's forward positions, having been in action from late afternoon until well into the evening, lacked the stomach for another major fight. However, to be fair, the German *Schwerpunkt* was still Hill 112 rather than the low ground.

11 July 1944 – Dawn on Hill 112

Back in the Orchard, a much reduced 5/DCLI had lost count of the number of counter-attacks that they had repulsed. Just before dawn word came that a squadron of Scots Greys was being sent in, to relieve the pressure on the Cornwalls, along with a company of Worcesters. During the night (02.00 hours) 1/Worcesters had come into the line to the east of 5/DCLI, having relieved the badly mauled 4/Wilts. The Scots Greys, of 4 Armoured Brigade, had remained south of Odon in support of the infantry on the lower slopes of Hill 112 and in front of Chateau de Fontaine. Lieutenant Franz Wallerstine, a troop commander with 7/RTR, has always wondered why the lightly armoured Shermans were sent up the Hill on the morning of 11 July 1944, rather than the more heavily protected Churchills. The answer is that the decision was made as 19 SS Panzer Grenadiers launched one of their counter-attacks and that B Squadron, Scots Greys, was to hand south of the river, while 7 RTR were leaguered up further to the north. The Cornwalls were pleased to have any support when 'The tanks arrived just before first light, cheering the men immensely'. Bringing them up was

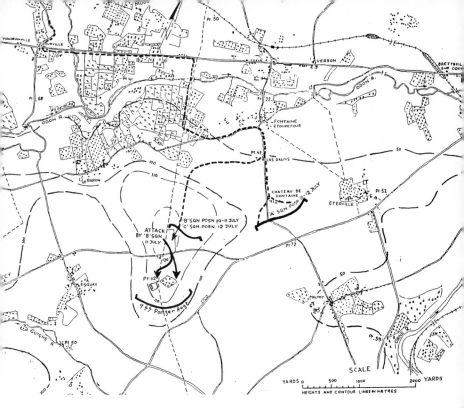

Captain Callender commanding B Squadron:

> 'There was now a considerable amount of chaos caused by a
> lot of tanks close together, with little space for manoeuvre. I went
> to see the infantry CO who was delighted we had arrived. I,
> personally, could see no reason to be pleased. AP shot and
> Spandau bullets were whistling through the wood. A heavy
> stonk wounded two tank commanders.'

Lieutenant Colonel James asked Captain Callender to drive the
enemy outposts out of the forward hedgerow. This was quickly
achieved but in doing so the Greys exposed themselves to
German anti-tank guns and armour on the southern edge of the
plateau and quickly lost five Shermans and a Royal Artillery
Sherman observation post tank. Captain Callender, his own
tank destroyed, recalls:

> 'The situation was now critical. The infantry could not
> possibly stand up to the terrific shelling and small arms fire for
> much longer. The noise was terriffic. My party was now reduced
> to four operational tanks and the infantry were suffering very
> heavy casualties.'

Knocked out Sherman in the orchard.

Attracting fire from every weapon in the 9th SS Panzer Division's 'ring of steel' around the southern slopes of Hill 112, orders for a withdrawal of the Greys soon came. Under cover of a smokescreen, the remaining operational Shermans withdrew back across the road into 4/Somerset LI's positions. The sacrifice of five tanks was counterbalanced by the destruction of up to nine enemy armoured fighting vehicles. B Squadron contributed significantly to the battle, although they did not appreciate it at the time, and were only on the Hill for a short period. At 07.20 hours the Commander of 9th SS Panzer Division, incorrectly believing that his division had 'solidly taken Hill 112', ordered that: '19 SS Panzer Grenadier Regiment are to hold Hill 112 with minimum strength. The remainder are to withdraw and dig in on the reverse slope out of sight of enemy ground observers'. The Germans had clearly decided to be more circumspect in the conduct of the battle. However, further counter-attacks were being prepared by 3/19 SS Panzer Grenadiers, well supported by the SS artillery regiments, in order to restore the frontline lost during the previous day's fighting.

Alone again on the Hill, 5/DCLI had to defend it in broad daylight against the series of attacks launched by 3/19 SS. While daylight brought the advantage to the counter-attacking Germans of more easily identifying their objective, it gave the defenders the opportunity of exploiting their superiority in artillery. Sergeant Frank Grigg's telephone line had been ripped up by the passage of both enemy and friendly tanks and Lieutenant Colonel James had to rely on his wireless set. Fortunately, a very good radio operator, Private Jack Foster, had joined him and the CO's normal operator Private Leslie Williams in the Orchard. Jack Foster describes some of his tasks early in the battle:

> 'During the initial advance, Leslie's set was damaged by shellfire, as were several of the company sets. Some of their signallers were wounded and our Lionel Blanchard was killed. During the battle Leslie, Luther and I were able to gather up three broken [No 18] sets and swap parts to make up a working set.'

No.18 Set with its canvas hood extended.

How well trained these signallers must have been to be able to carry out such a complex task in the dark and under fire! A passage from Jack Foster's Military Medal citation gives a feel for the night's action:

> 'For several hours, the Coys were cut off from [Main] Battalion Headquarters by enemy tanks and infantry having infiltrated the position. The line communication had been cut and several 18-sets and signallers had been knocked out. During this time communication was effected by the remaining 18-set manned by Private Foster J. The enemy was frequently so close that he had to whisper in order to get his vital calls for artillery fire and ammunition supplies through, and at all times was under heavy fire and it was impossible for him to raise himself above ground level. By his steadiness and devotion to duty a continuous stream of messages directing artillery fire on to enemy concentrations was received at [Main] Bn HQ, many counter-attacks were broken up and severe casualties inflicted on the enemy.'

In daylight, his skills were to be tested to the full. Lieutenant Colonel James wanted to make the most of the opportunity to

Trees surrounding the orchard were shredded by artillery fire.

use artillery to keep the Germans at bay. He climbed a tree that had been badly blasted during the previous twenty-four hours of battle. From his elevated position, he could see over the hedges and slightly downhill onto the German positions. Calling down map references, Jack Foster, with his precious radio in a trench below, passed them back to be relayed to the guns of 94/Field Regiment. The CO had the pleasure of seeing the Germans pull back under heavy and accurate fire just before he was spotted. A burst of Spandau fire ripped through the tree. 'Come down sir!' shouted Jack Foster. The Colonel replied 'I am coming' but he was too late, as a second burst shot him out of the tree. He fell, almost decapitated, by the side of Private Foster. Word spread from trench to trench that 'The CO's had it' and in the words of George Taylor, who took over command the following day,

'Now with the Colonel dead the splendid fighting spirit that had sustained the battalion through many hours of grim and deadly struggle began to wane. Someone shouted: "Retreat! Retreat!" Who it was will ever remain a mystery. ...Men began

to drift to the rear and the contagion spread and considerable numbers reached the position held by 4th Somersets, where the latter's Colonel, CG Lipscombe, rallied them.'

Majors Fry and Roberts led the remains of the Cornwalls back to their positions in the Orchard. Overcoming fear to return to battle from a position of relative safety is a measure of true bravery. The soldiers were reorganized into four 'companies' which were in fact only the strength of platoons.

Meanwhile, back in 4/Somerset LI's position, Major John Majendie recalls that Lieutenant Colonel Lipscombe,

'sensing a crisis drew his pistol and shouted "I'll shoot the first Somerset who goes back." And an honest private soldier in my company told me, years later, "When I saw the DCLI coming I put on my small pack and if they had gone I would have gone with them."

Corporal DB Jones, one of the ten percent of a unit 'left out of battle' in case of disaster had come forward to join his Battalion just after 5/DCLI's return to the Orchard.

'I was astonished to see Lippy and the Brigadier sitting on shooting sticks apparently discussing the battle, as bullets were flying all around. A sergeant I came up with was killed but still they sat there! They were sitting there regardless of their safety! I now know why they were doing it but they earned our respect and affection.'

Morale of fighting men in battle can be a fragile thing and, as George Taylor said, the 'contagion' could spread quickly. Helped by the calm heroism of their brigadier and some brave leadership by officers and NCOs of the two battalions, 43rd Wessex were saved from embarrassment.

Back on the Hill, 5/DCLI were subjected to further counter-attacks but the attacks lessened in both frequency and intensity as the combat power of the two sides ebbed away. Incidents of the utmost ferocity were juxtaposed with ones of compassion or simple 'live and let live'. For example, an artillery Forward Observation Officer remembers: 'I said "There's a Jerry over there" and I raised my rifle to have a bang at him but the chap whose trench I was sharing said "Don't shoot at him, you'll annoy them".' However, SS-*Mann* Trautmann, on the eastern edge of the Small Wood recalls another side to the battle:

'On our left was an enclosure where our opponents were trying to bring an anti-tank gun into action. The crew was

A knocked out Mark IV on Hill 112.

frantically pulling down the fence ... Brave were those Anglo-Saxons but we were rapidly closing on them so their efforts were meaningless; they would never be ready to fire in time. We quickly made the manhandling of that dark-brown gun a superfluous exercise. The gun was literally dismantled by our shot, with shield flying through the air and wheels hurled across the field. The Tommies screamed, throwing their arms in the air as they died, or somersaulted, horribly mutilated.'

SS-*Sturmmann* Herbert Furbringer of 19 SS Panzer Grenadiers, has described how he,

'... was wounded about 300 yards beyond Hill 112. I just failed to make it into a ditch and was badly wounded in one leg by a British shell. I handed my ammunition over to my comrades, who I never saw again, and started to hobble down the Roman Road. I came upon a wounded British soldier, leaning against a bank. I raised my rifle and shouted to him to put his hands up. He swore at me and I realized the stupidity of the situation and we hobbled back together down to my Regiment's aid post.'

Major John Majendie recalls meeting one of the *Hohenstaufen's* stretcher-bearers at the fiftieth anniversary commemorations of the battle. He told of how he was sent into the Orchard to collect wounded, who were within a short distance of a British tank but 'despite traversing its turret towards us, to their eternal credit, they did not fire'.

152

In the early afternoon, there was a lull in the battle and Major Roberts, one of two surviving company commanders, took the opportunity to visit the positions:

'To give some idea of how depleted the battalion had become, just before I was wounded I made a tour of the companies and the effective strength was 126, although many of the wounded were still lying where they had fallen or been hit in their slit trenches: some were still firing, although very weak for loss of blood and fatigue.'

At about 15.00 hours the respite ended in a fury of shot and shell that raked the hilltop. The SS were mounting yet another counter-attack, this time with the support of the *Stug* VIs of 9/SS Assault-gun Battalion. Reinforced by fresh troops, the *Hohenstaufen* was starting to make progress. Realizing that they were about to be overrun, Major Fry requested permission to withdraw but he only received a curt order to 'return to the brigade commander and explain the situation'. As the sole surviving officer, the burden of making the decision to order an unauthorized withdrawal now, or to await the deliberations of the chain of command, fell on Major Fry. It is almost certain that

SS-Standartenführer Sander at his command post in Bully. From here he commanded the fire of the *Frundsberg's* artillery support throughout the battle.

after fourteen days in the forward battle area and twenty-one hours in action on Hill 112, 5/DCLI would have been destroyed if Major Fry had not ordered a prompt withdrawal.

Thus Operation JUPITER came to a close with about sixty men of 5/DCLI coming down from the Hill, with others straggling in over succeeding hours and days. The Battalion's losses were eventually calculated as two hundred and fifty-four including twenty-six shell shock cases. The battle had also reduced the enemy's capabilities significantly, with some SS Panzer Grenadier companies reduced to an effective strength of five or six men.

Hill 112 had not been held, nor had the Orne crossings been seized but elements of no less than four SS panzer divisions had been engaged in battle and firmly fixed on the British front at a vital point in the campaign. In doing so II SS Panzer Corps was so heavily written down that it never recovered to anything like the level of combat power it was able to deploy at dawn on 10 July 1944. In summary, Operation JUPITER may not have been a tactical success for Major General Thomas but it was a strategic success for Montgomery.

Put up by 5/DCLI in the days following the battle.

CHAPTER FIVE

THE CAPTURE OF MALTOT
AND THE FALL OF HILL 112

'In these conditions, comparable only in the writer's experience to the bombardment at Passchendaele, the Division was to remain in action for a further fourteen days.'

Brigadier H Essame. 214 Brigade

With Operation JUPITER over and preparations still underway for Operation GOODWOOD, Hill 112 had lost none of its importance to both the British and the Germans. All along the front from Hill 112 to Tilly and beyond, Montgomery's overarching strategic aim was still to keep the German panzer formations firmly fixed on the British front, while the Americans attempted to break out. Within Second British Army, XII Corps was now tasked to maintain pressure on Hill 112 and the area to the south-west. This was designed to keep German reserves tied down and to distract attention from the area where Operation GOODWOOD was to be launched to the east of Caen, a week later. At the tactical level, both sides made limited attacks and counter-attacks to gain ground and improve their positions. On Hill 112, both sides were clinging to the edges of the plateau, peering covetously from their slit trenches at the fire-swept ruins of the Orchard a few hundred metres away.

At this stage, the British armoured divisions were being prepared for GOODWOOD and only the independent tank and armoured brigades were available to support attacks. The run-down strength of infantry battalions was also shaping conduct of operations. Both sides had suffered heavy casualties during EPSOM, the capture of Caen and Carpiquet, and during Operation JUPITER. The infantry depots in Britain and Germany were emptying rapidly and, after nearly five years of war, there was no realistic chance of them filling again. The pool of SS replacements was nearly exhausted and discussions about taking lower quality *Wehrmacht* recruits into the elite SS formations were under way. The British had planned a mobile battle with the tank taking centre stage and had trained too few infantry battle casualty replacements. Consequently, Montgomery faced the prospect of breaking up divisions to keep others up to strength, while at home recruits were directed to the infantry training regiments. Reversing the conversions of 1942, artillerymen and even RAF conscripts would soon be retrained as infantrymen. All this would take time, so in the meantime economy of effort was the watchword along the British front. Attacks were, therefore, to be on a relatively small scale.

The following sections illustrate selected incidents during the period from 11 July until Maltot and Hill 112 were eventually taken in August. They give a feel for what it was like to be in action on a piece of 'vital ground' before the breakout.

4/Som LI attempt to grab the Hill

War diary and signal log of Panzer Group West (Eberbach) to II SS Panzer Corps (Bittrich).

> '21.30 hours 11 Jul 44. On no account must Hill 112 be given up: it is the pivot of the whole front. We might be able to do without Eterville but we must hang on to Hill 112.'

Shortly after receipt of this message, the British were to mount a small-scale attack designed to grab positions on the crest of Hill 112. The attack by 4/Somerset LI took place as darkness fell on the evening of 11 July 1944. The operation was to be 'silent'; that is to say that there was to be no preliminary bombardment and 4/Somerset LI were to advance as far as possible without alerting the enemy. Only when the attack had 'gone noisy' would the artillery, mortars and machine guns join the battle.

Major John Majendie describes A Company's supporting role in the advance:

> 'At about dusk on the second night we were just starting to dig new positions for some of my company to get away from the very vulnerable Roman Road, when we received orders that three of our companies under the direct instructions of the Brigade Commander were to advance forward to try to establish positions on the higher ground of the hill. C Company on the left, D in the centre and my own Company [A] on the right. It was a fairly impromptu affair, we advanced forward in the dark and established ourselves with two platoons forward of the road and

German M42 general purpose machine gun.

one behind it and we then started to dig in. The ground there was twice as hard as the ground we had come from, we had shovels but few picks with which to dig. To add to the problems while we were starting to dig our own medium machine guns opened up on the Boche from behind us and in reply two or three Spandaus started firing into my company's position. We had some casualties and were obliged to try to dig lying on our sides because the tracer was zipping just over our heads. I sent my 2IC back to tell the CO that I didn't think that we would be down below ground level before it was light.'

In the centre, D Company had the main task: to occupy the Orchard. John Majendie was watching:

'D Company had advanced forward pretty well to the edge of Cornwall Wood and ran straight into trouble. A lot of machine-gun fire and a lot of bullets were ricocheting off knocked out tanks and were causing casualties. One of their platoons veered off to the right and wasn't seen again.'

Opposing 4/Somerset LI was SS-*Mann* Hans Greiesinger of 19th SS Panzer Grenadiers who had crept forward to a position just to the east of the Orchard:

'We were on the left next to the shell shattered Kastenwäldschen. Tommy came twice in the darkness with shock troops but we were able to drive him off. One of the attackers was hit and burned to death before he could get his flamethrower going. We tried to contact our neighbours on the other side of the

*Kastenwäldschen but we found no one there. They had cleared off
without telling us.'*

It is almost certain that Hans Greiesinger had mistaken the
explosions of a phosphorus grenade for that of a man pack
flame thrower. These vulnerable devices were in common use in
the SS pioneer battalions but not in the British Army. A British
observer saw and heard what happened to a soldier in D
Company to his front:

*'We saw ahead of us a brilliant flash of light 200 to 300 yards
ahead of us. We wondered what it was at the time and we
afterwards heard that some poor private soldier had been hit in
the stomach by machine gun fire and a phosphorus grenade in
his pouch set him alight. He was lying on the ground, with no
hope at all. One of the officers was there and he said to him
'Please sir, shoot me' and the officer shot him and the soldier said
'No sir, not there, in the head', which was done.'*

Hill 112 as No Man's Land

On headquarters' map boards, red and blue chinagraph
pencil 'duck eggs' marked both British and enemy positions.
Commanders, peering at the contours in the dim light of
paraffin lamps saw that the hilltop was most definitely No
Man's Land. It was far too important for either side to let the
other hold, as possession would enable observers to see deep
into opposition territory. Artillery, mortar and machine-gun fire
swept through the Orchard and effectively
denied the area of the crest to infantry of
both the Wessex Division and II SS Panzer
Corps. On the plateau's northern and
southern slopes, casualties mounted as
bombardments of potential attackers'
forming-up points became a regular feature
of daily life. If, however, commanders
thought that the Orchard was unoccupied,
they were wrong. Sheltering in dugouts
and under knocked-out armoured vehicles
were small groups of soldiers. Private
Gordon Mucklow was one of them.

Gordon Mucklow

*'Sometime during the next day we moved
forward to take up positions on the
[forward] edge of the orchard. There didn't*

Allied aerial photograph taken 6 July 1944 and marked with the position of the British front line after Operation JUPITER.

seem to be so many of our lot about and we were short of ammunition. Someone volunteered to get some ammunition and quite soon appeared with a canvas bag of loose .303 rounds. We divided it up between us. We knew we could hold our own and wondered why we were not being supported and hadn't had any compo packs [ration packs of tinned food]. I suppose we had been four days without food or water, and having survived so far became adventurous. We did wonder if we could use the abandoned anti-tank gun lying in the corner of the Orchard. None of us knew how, which was just as well as the firing mechanism had been taken out during the retreat.

'We had not been shelled for a while and we decided to find out what was on the other side of the hedge. Some, groping around, discovered a hole in the ground far deeper than any we had managed to shelter in at night (we had spent the previous night under a Sherman tank). Before I was prepared to enter this dugout, I fired a burst from my Bren. Imagine my surprise when out popped four Jerries with their hands above their heads

159

shouting something we didn't understand. One of us volunteered to march them back rather too quickly and we feared that we might be in trouble for not searching them.

'Later that day a runner came into the orchard saying "What in hell are you doing here? The order came to retreat days ago!" It didn't take us long to pull out! We must have looked a motley lot, not having shaved for days and stinking of rotting corpses.'

Such was the determination and self confidence of the opposing infantry, that small groups of resolute men held positions despite a lack of orders.

The Scots and Welch at le Bon Repos.

The capture of the cross roads at le Bon Repos (The Good Rest!) and the hills overlooking Esquay was a subsidiary attack designed to secure the left flank of a larger operation to the west. On the evening of 15 July, 2/Glasgow Highlanders were to launch their attack against positions held by 3/21 SS Panzer Grenadiers, organized in only three companies due to their losses during EPSOM. However, they were generously supported by the Churchills of 107/Regiment RAC, and by 79th Armoured Division's 'Funnies' in the form of the Armoured Vehicles Royal Engineers (AVREs) with their demolition guns and the more familiar Crocodiles. 1/Middlesex were also on call with their heavy mortars and machine guns to add to the weight of fire available to the Glasgow Highlanders.

The attack was to come from the north-east across the lower slopes of Hill 112. A Company on the right was to advance up to the road and wheel right to follow it down to le Bon Repos. B and D Companies were to fight through the German outposts on the south-west slopes of Hill 112 and head for their objectives in Esquay.

The divisional history of 15th Scottish Division describes how, as they emerged from the low ground, the attackers were,

'...greeted with a storm of mortar fire which temporarily threw the battalion out of control. To make matters worse, the very welcome smoke-screen which our guns were putting down on Point 112 and the slopes to the south-west of it, had turned into fog which was obscuring the whole area. In

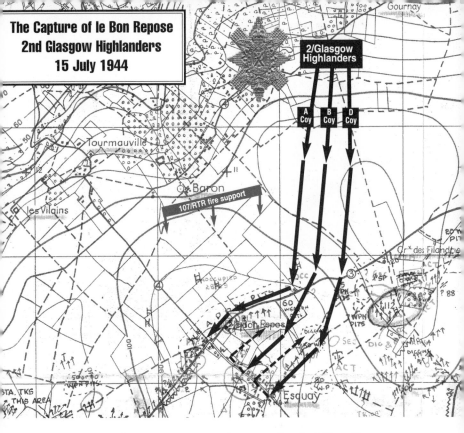

The Capture of le Bon Repose
2nd Glasgow Highlanders
15 July 1944

consequence there was a proper mix up on the start line. None
the less A and B Companies managed to cross it on time at 9.30
p.m.

'From that point the attack went without a hitch. First the
Crocodiles did their stuff, quickly burning the enemy garrison
out of the entrenchments dug along the road between le Bon
Repos and the Croix des Filandriers. The survivors
surrendered...'

The advance continued down the slope, illuminated by Monty's
Moonlight: the diffused beams of searchlights reflected off the
clouds. The Churchills, firing HE from the ridge into the village
below, continued the work that the artillery had started in
numbing the defenders. Round after round of HE was fired into
any likely enemy position in Esquay. The Glasgow Highlanders
had completed clearing the village by 23.00 hours but,

'They had no intention of occupying it, however. Down in the
bottom of a saucer, Esquay was nothing but a shell-trap.

Esquay   le Bon Repos   A Coy

D and B Coy

Companies at once moved out to consolidate the area on the surrounding slopes, which Lieutenant Colonel Campbell had already allocated to them on air photographs. Thus the Glasgow Highlanders were now positioned for their task of protecting the left flank of the main attack.'

It is clear from German records that the Glasgow Highlander's activity between the Croix des Filandriers and le Bon Repos also had the effect of making the Germans believe that the British were mounting a new major assault on Hill 112. They deployed the Tigers up the hill into the smoke, where they sat inactive while the battle developed to the west. The main attack of Operation GREENLINE is not within the scope of this book's geographical area but suffice it to say that 15th Scottish Division gained a tenuous hold on Point 113 but failed to take Evrecy. Consequently, the Glasgow Highlanders found themselves in exposed positions between Hill 112 and Point 113, which no amount of smoke could render safe for movement above ground level. Overlooked at le Bon Repos and around Esquay, they were constantly shelled while the enemy wasted a lot of time, energy and resources engaging non-existent positions in Esquay. The repeated counter-attacks, mounted by 5 Company 1/10 SS Panzer Regiment and Grenadiers from 1 and 2 Companies 21 SS Panzer Grenadier Regiment, came only after the main British attack had been 'controlled'. Initially, A Company at le Bon Repos was the focus of most attention. Sergeant Jimmy Blair's section of 6-pounder anti-tank guns stood their ground and kept firing despite seeing shells bounce

Sergeant Jimmy Blair

off the approaching enemy tanks' armour. Eventually, the Mark IVs got so close that the 6-pounders' last shots penetrated the frontal armour of the two leading tanks at almost point-blank range. On other occasions the Glasgow Highlander's forward platoons were forced to withdraw, returning to their original position only after the SS infantry's counter-attack had been broken by the medium guns of the Royal Artillery.

After two days under fire the Glasgow Highlanders were relieved from their unenviably exposed positions by 5/Welch from 53rd Welsh Division. On 21 July 1944, 10th SS Panzer Division made a determined attack on the le Bon Repos crossroads from where the British could see down the valley between the key features of Hill 112 and Point 113. Driving 5/Welch and their supporting artillery observers back over the ridge would greatly improve the German positions. Sergeant Jim Machin, with Battalion Headquarters in the Intelligence Section, describes the attack:

'These are unforgettable moments when the whole front leaps into violent life. These are moments of agony, of drama, of heroic deeds, which nothing will ever erase from living memory.

'At 16.00hrs A Coy 5/Welch commanded by Major Nethercott reported being attacked by four tanks. The enemy – SS troops – had attacked our right forward company at le Bon Repos with the intention of over-running it and then turning right to roll up the whole of our forward defences.

'At 18.00hrs, a platoon of B Coy holding a left forward position was over-run by enemy tanks and infantry. At 19.30hrs two squadrons of our tanks opened up with their Besas in the general direction of le Bon Repos church. Despite urgent DF [Defensive Fire] tasks fired by the divisional artillery the SS troops pressed on. They killed two stretcher bearers with a four foot square Red Cross flag, trying to save a wounded tankman. At 20.00hrs A Coy reported tanks fifty yards away from their positions. The last communication came at 21.30hrs by which time A Coy had been totally swamped and were entirely lost.'

Lieutenant Mostyn Thomas, commander of 18 Platoon, recalls:

'Observation became poor due to smoke and debris. LMG fire cracked over us and thudded into the ground. Tanks could be seen and our artillery response was heavy. It was bedlam. Jerry rolled up the front,'A' Coy went down in the late evening.

We were submerged in German mortar and artillery fire when their infantry advanced. Ian Evans's voice came over loud and clear repeatedly saying 'Get your heads up'. Heads did come up but I was caught by a Nebelwerfer which exploded to my right.'

Sergeant Machin again:

'As night fell the battered forward line contracted into the area of 'C' Coy under Major JH Morgan. Permission to vacate the top of Baron Hill was denied until 06.00hrs in the morning when the remnants of 5/Welch retired under cover of smoke. Private George won the DCM for knocking out an enemy tank.'

The battle at le Bon Repos cost 5/Welch a total of one hundred and forty killed, wounded and missing. The Churchill tanks sent to help them had been totally out-gunned by the six Tigers that worked their way around the western slope of Hill 112 to support the SS infantry. Despite the fire support of the entire corps artillery, which is difficult to fully utilize once close quarter combat is joined, the enemy were able to fight their way through the 53rd Welsh Division's positions around le Bon Repos.

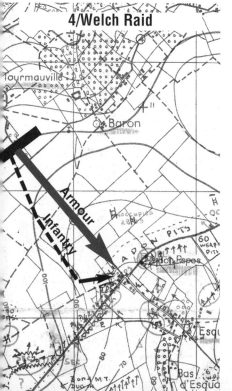

On the evening of 23 July, 4/Welch set out in force to raid the German positions at le Bon Repos. Supported by the divisional artillery and six Crocodiles, two companies of Welshmen attacked the Germans in their sister battalion's old positions. In half an hour's blood-letting, fuelled by weeks of frustration, 2/21 SS Panzer Grenadiers were badly mauled and their morale seriously undermined. The battle on the British front had become one of attrition.

164

129 Brigade's attack on Maltot.

Before the Wessex Division left the Odon/Orne battlefield, they were given one last attack: Operation EXPRESS. Maltot had been the Operation JUPITER objective of 7/Hampshires and 4/Dorsets. Both of these battalions had suffered cruelly in the attempt to take and hold the village. Twelve days later, the same task was to fall to 4 and 5/Wilts.

To describe Maltot as a village would be wrong. The fighting of 10 July 1944, and the subsequent bickering exchanges of artillery and mortar fire had reduced the village to rubble. Infantrymen of German 272nd Infantry Division, who arrived by foot from the Pas de Calais, now held the rubble pile of Maltot. Less potent than an SS panzer division, these were none the less experienced soldiers who had been blooded on the Eastern Front. By 22 July, the German infantrymen had taken over 10 SS Panzer Division's defensive positions, built into the ruins of the village. Forcing them out of the rubble would not be an easy task. Elements of 10th SS Panzer Division had moved back into reserve in the St Martin area, in a counter-attack role.

The plan for Operation EXPRESS was simple and limited in scope: the attack was to come from the north-east along the bottom of the Orne Valley with the river on the attackers' left. On 10 July, 130 Brigade and 9/RTR had attacked across the open ground south of Chateau Fontaine and Eterville, which had been overlooked by anti-tank guns on Hill 112. The divisional artillery and the medium guns of two AGRAs pounded 130 Brigade's objectives. The new attack was to be astride the road from Louvigny. 5/Wilts and B Squadron 7/RTR were

Ruined houses in Maltot.

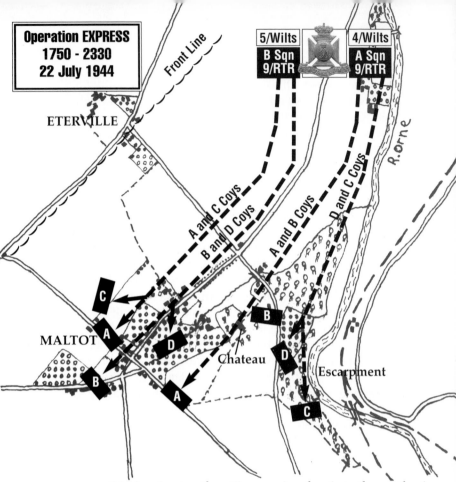

responsible for clearing the village and orchards to the north of the road, while 4/Wilts with A Squadron were to attack the woods, orchards and spur to the south-east of the village. The task of clearing these woods was complicated by the presence of defended quarries and caves in the area of the Escarpment, on the banks of the Orne. 4/Som LI were in reserve, ready to exploit success.

5/Wilts

The attack started at 17.30 hours and progressed well for 5/Wilts who had a fairly clear run to the village. Their history describes how:

> *'They made an impressive sight as they surged forward through the tall corn widely deployed but moving steadily on, for all the world as though they were on a parade ground. Ahead, a*

smoke screen had been laid, and into it crashed our artillery barrage.

'The enemy were undoubtedly caught by surprise, nevertheless by the time the rear companies had followed the leading companies across the start line, the enemy were retaliating with shell and mortar fire amongst the advancing troops.'

Once in the village, 5/Wilts found the German defenders initially stunned by the ferocity of the British artillery fire. As the Wiltshires penetrated into Maltot the enemy recovered and the defence became more dogged. As ammunition ran low, hand-to-hand fighting became the norm. During the battle, Private Long formed a low opinion of German bayonet fighting:

'They would come rushing at you like wild bulls, with bayonet raised above their heads; all we had to do was wait for them, parry their bayonets to one side, up with our rifle butt to smash their jaws and then as they fell stick them.'

The *Wehrmacht* infantry may have been surprised, but the SS were fully prepared for the Wiltshires' attack. 102/SS Heavy Panzer Regiment and Grenadiers from 10th SS Panzer Division were already counter-attacking as the British entered Maltot. The Tigers advanced through the 43rd Wessex Division's barrage and met the tanks of 7/RTR coming in the opposite

Churchills advancing through standing corn in the Caen area.

direction. SS-*Mann* Trautmann, gunner in a Tiger of 1st Company has written that:

> '*The voice of the tank commander crackled on the set 'Half left – 500'. Looking left as the turret swung around I could see four tanks coming down the road towards us. Long hull, small, short turret – Churchills. Then came the fire order 'Targets – the leading tank and the rear tank, fire!' The first Churchill blocked the road, the crew baling out. The rear tank soon burned. The two in the middle were trapped. Number three gets hit twice in succession in the hull – nobody gets out of that one. The last one is hit in the stern, white smoke comes out of the hatches and then the ammunition explodes, a sheet of flame leaps from the engine and the heavy plates fly into the air.*'

The signals officer, Captain John McMath, recalls the bravery of one of his signallers who rescued the dismounted armoured soldiers:

> '*Private Cooling dressed the tank crew's wounds as they lay on the road amid bursting shells from the tanks. One by one he lifted six badly wounded men onto a Jeep and drove through the rubble back to the RAP.*'

Luckily for the Wyverns, the Tigers' intervention in Maltot was mercifully brief. A British Forward Air Controller saw the enemy tanks coming down the slope to the west and had called up the RAF Typhoons from the 'cab rank' of aircraft circling above, off the coast. The German counter-attack was quickly halted and the Tigers fled back to positions on the south-west ridge of Hill 112. Grenadiers from 10 SS Panzer Division joined their *Wehrmacht* colleagues in Maltot's rubble as welcome reinforcements.

The taste of success, confirmed by the sight of the dreaded Tigers withdrawing, was sweet on the tongues of the Wiltshiremen, especially as it followed the losses in the bitter JUPITER battles twelve days earlier. Initial success was a crucial element in maintaining the forward momentum that took the 5/Wilts and B Squadron through the enemy positions, blasting enemy infantry out of the rubble as they went. As small arms ammunition and the all-important grenades ran out, Corporal Wiltshire resorted to knocking Germans out by hurling tins of bully beef at them. Surely the most unusual house clearing weapons ever.

5/Wilts were clearly on a roll. Towards the end of their battle, Captain 'Abe' Lincoln, the charismatic commander of B Company and fluent German speaker, calmly walked up to one of a platoon of assault guns (*Stug* IVs from 10th SS Panzer Division). Holding up his hand, he imperiously demanded to speak to the commander who, with a look of incredulity, popped up out of his hatch and was invited to surrender! This was a popular idea with the gun crews. However, negotiations were interrupted by salvos of shells from the British 5.5in guns that sent Captain Lincoln diving for cover and the Germans motoring back to the safety of Hill 112 as fast as they could.

4/Wilts

On the south side of the road, 4/Wilts had to fight their way through a wooded area and clear some outlying farms before reaching their objectives south of Maltot. Their war diary gives an indication of the lower level tactics.

> '*H-Hour 17.30 – Bn moved with two coys up, C Coy left, A Coy right – res[erve] D Coy left, B Coy right. Because of the close nature of the ground one tank moved with each platoon – Two sects [sections each of 8 – 10 men] of each pl leading and one sect moving close to the tank as its bodyguard against bazookas, sticky grenades, etc, which might be fired from amongst the woods and houses – co-operation by the tanks was very good.*'

Clearly protecting the tanks, which were especially vulnerable to attack in close country and villages, was a priority if the infantry were to enjoy the firepower of the tanks' machine guns and main armament. Working closely or 'co-operating' with the

infantry, the tanks would blast the enemy out of their defences, thus considerably reducing the risks inherent to the infantry in an unsupported attack in the close country. To ensure proper coordination with the infantry, squadron commanders went into battle on foot alongside the infantry commanding officers. This resulted in swift, effective decision making. One early result was that the squadron commander who saw that A Company 4/Wilts had been held up on the open approaches to Lieu de la France, at the eastern end of Maltot, quickly organized tank support. His headquarters' tanks brought up the Crocodiles and, together with HE, flame and machine-gun fire, made short work of the German defenders. The advance continued.

William Biles, a private with a platoon headquarters, describes an incident early in C Company's attack:

'We were told to take a small house in the wood, only five Jerries inside, easy. ...As I walked up the road all I could see through the foliage was the top windows and part of the front door. Number 3 Section got the job of actually assaulting, and as they tore up the path, a machine gun fired a short burst and wounded two of them. One managed to crawl away but the other chap was hit in the stomach. So our Red Cross bloke put a big red

Crocodiles in action.

cross on the end of a bayonet and held it out where the Germans could see it. There was no firing so he crawled out; then they fired and hit him in the leg. So it was decided to call up the tank from the rear. But I had the bright idea, as I was Number One of the 2in mortar, to fire HE on the house. My mate opened up the case, and I lay down behind the mortar and poked it in the general direction of the front door; I'd never fired the thing before, so I was hoping for the best! "Well, Bill, I'll bung em in and you fire 'em" said the Sergeant. I pulled the handle but when the first one hit, it didn't explode, it just poured smoke. "They're not bloody HE, they're smoke rounds," yelled the Sergeant. "Never mind," he said, "we'll use those while he's opening the bloody HE." So he was putting 'em down the barrel, and I was letting 'em off, when I hears a rat-tat-tat right behind me head. It was our tank, firing into the house, which was covered in thick white smoke. Hell of a din! Then they raided the house and instead of five coming out, there was forty-five.'

In the woods, the fighting was short, sharp and bloody. The deadly game of cat and mouse through the trees, quarries and trenches strained the infantry's every nerve. Those who fought the battle lost all sense of time. However, the artillery records indicate that the bulk of the task was completed within two hours. Mopping up and securing gains, as usual, took longer but as light faded one last German position remained unsubdued. The enemy had withdrawn to Chateau Maltot in 4/Wilts' area to make their final defence, despite being cut off as the advancing companies bypassed the strong point.

By 19.00 hours, it was clear that the Chateau had become a problem. As they moved up from reserve to take the lead along the banks of the small Rau de Maltot and up onto the ridge to the south-east of Maltot, B Company came under heavy fire from the upper floors. The enemy had halted the advance in its tracks. B Company's accompanying troop of tanks was brought forward and started to soften up the defenders; however, the strongly built Chateau seemed to absorb the HE shells and Besa machine-gun fire. After a while a *Wehrmacht* medic came out of the chateau bearing a flag of truce and requested that they be allowed to evacuate the growing number of wounded. His request was refused, unless all the defenders came out and surrendered. Unable to accept these terms, the German medic returned to the Chateau and the battle resumed. At dusk,

The Chateau, last position of the German defenders at Maltot, and the same building today.

Lieutenant Rutherford's 18 Platoon assaulted the Chateau with tanks moving as close as they dared to help the assaulting infantry break into the Chateau. 18 Platoon gained entry to the ground floor, which they largely cleared, but were subsequently subjected to a hail of grenades thrown down the stairwells and through holes in the ceiling. Sergeant Eyer led a charge up the main stairs, but in the now almost complete darkness, they were beaten back. During the course of the night, the outbuildings were steadily cleared and the main Chateau received the regular attention of the tanks.

Despite the continuing resistance at the Chateau, both 4 and 5/Wilts reported that, between 21.30 and 22.00 hours, they had successfully reached their objectives on the western edge of Maltot and the woods to the south. The two 7/RTR squadrons were released at 22.30 by the grateful Wiltshires. Having lost eight tanks, they now returned to leaguers behind the start line. Back in Maltot, as darkness fell, the battle started to die down, but it was not until shortly after first light the following morning that the Germans in the Chateau surrendered. Private Main was detailed to escort the prisoners to the Brigade POW collection point:

> '*There was one bloke who spoke good English. He told me that they had held out thinking that the SS would counter-attack and rescue them and when no attack came at dawn, the Major faced the inevitable and surrendered before the Chateau was blown down bit by bit. Apparently, there had been some discussion about the risk of surrendering as some had seen what happened to prisoners in Russia.*'

The inevitable German counter-attack failed to materialize; clearly a sign that weeks of battle had taken its toll on the enemy. 10th SS Panzer Division was reduced from 15,000 men to just 2,289. Only the most important positions were to be counter-attacked, despite what Hitler demanded in Berlin. Maltot was lost but the British were contained below the ridges of Hill 112, with its dug-in tanks and guns.

Daylight revealed that the infantry had an unpleasant surprise to deal with. Captain Robbins, who had in the previous week taken over as adjutant of 4/Wilts, recounts:

> '*we didn't realize that 130 Brigade had been put into Maltot and had been virtually written off during Jupiter. We saw their destroyed vehicles and the rotting bodies scattered around the village. It doesn't take long for a body to rot in the hot sun.*'

Some of the upwards of 400 prisoners taken during the fighting at Maltot. These veterans of the Russian Front are all holders of the Iron Cross.

Main Street, Maltot then and now.

As a stretcher bearer with B Company Headquarters, Private Geoff White describes a harrowing task in understated terms;

'Another duty we had to perform was burying the dead Dorsets and Hampshires. This wasn't very nice, especially as you were looking out for the next shell. Burying the bodies and wondering when you were going to join them isn't fun!'

Outside the village the German panzers and anti-tank guns fired down into Maltot from the south-east ridge of Hill 112, which made life very unpleasant for the British infantry. The attack had been well prepared and very well executed by two battalions who had been schooled in the cauldron of battle. It is with some justifiable pride that the Wiltshires claim that their capture of Maltot was 'a text book operation'. Over four hundred prisoners from 272nd Infantry and 10th SS Panzer Divisions had been taken.

The End at Hill 112.

On 30 July 1944, the British breakout-from the lodgement began, but it was not where the Germans expected it to be. They had been preparing to resume their defence of Hill 112 and the line of the River Orne. However, in the preceding days, the centre of gravity of the British Second Army had been transferred to the western flank alongside the Americans who were beginning to forge south. The lateral passage of lines (crossing through the rear of other divisions) by units grouped under XXX Corps was a marvellously executed piece of staff work, showing considerable discipline and training in one of the most difficult phases of war. By the early hours of 1 August 1944, II SS Panzer Corps vehicles were streaming away from Hill 112 to the new crisis point in the area of Mont Pincon. Here they would again meet their old adversaries – the 43rd Wessex and 15th Scottish Divisions – in a mobile battle of an entirely different character from that fought between the Rivers Odon and Orne.

Replacing 43rd Wessex on Hill 112 was the 53rd Welsh Division which, in the relatively quiet conditions, was able to expand its area of responsibility to take over the frontage formerly held by the two divisions. As increasing numbers of Germans were drawn to face the breakout in the south-west, the Recce Regiment of the Welsh Division was able to slip through the le Bon Repos crossroads:

'We crept over the brow of the hill at zero hour to see a large open expanse of shell-potted ground with many knocked out tanks and vehicles scattered about. My first thought was whether my [armoured] car would add to this collection. I had never felt so frightened before. Our progress was slow but we edged down the narrow road, dodging a demolished carrier and bumping over shell holes. There was a road barrier 300 yds ahead, which I kept well covered with my Bren. Despite mines cleared by the assault troop, A Sqn got into the shell torn village of Esquay. C Sqn advanced on the right and reached the River Orne at Pont de Coudray after an amazing advance of five to six miles in the wake of the retreating enemy!'

As the centre of events moved westwards, the advantageous and remarkable views from Hill 112 lost their relevance. On 4 August 1944, after all the blood spilt down its slopes, Hill 112 fell into the hands of 53rd Welsh Division with hardly a fight.

Let the words of War Minister Sir James Griggs's report to the House of Commons have the final say on the six weeks of fighting at Hill 112:

*'Meanwhile, the British and Canadians, though making some local gains, were primarily concerned with holding the hinge position south-west of Caen and containing the greater part of the enemy's available armour. **To them had been assigned the unspectacular task of forming the anvil upon which the German Forces were held and pounded to destruction.'***

Chapter Six

TOURS OF THE HILL 112 BATTLEFIELD

The tour described here will enable the visitor to travel around the main scenes of action in the Hill 112 battle area. It is assumed that the visitor will have transport, be it minibus, car or bicycle. However, there are a couple of parts of the battlefield that can only be visited on foot and are included in the tour itinerary described below. This combination of vehicle and foot will cater for most tastes.

The tour starts in the Odon Valley between the villages of Verson and Fontaine Etoupefour. Most visitors will approach the area from the Caen area or more likely from the city's *Peripherique* autoroute. For those setting out from the centre of Caen you should head for the western outskirts and the *Peripherique*. **From the Peripherique take exit nine** and join the **D 675**, signposted **Rennes** and **Verson**. Follow the signs around the roundabouts towards Verson. Four hundred metres after the roundabout the road forks downhill to the left. **Take the D 214**, signposted to **Fontaine Etoupefou**r. At the **Verson church** follow the road to the left. **Pause** by the **bridge** across the River Odon.

DEATH VALLEY ➊ (see map on page 178)

You are at the bottom of the Odon Valley or what became known to the Wessex Division as 'Death Valley'. This unspectacular stream was an obstacle to both wheeled and tracked movement. The watercourse is quite deep and steep-sided, with the tree-lined banks providing further problems. This bridge was in No Man's Land on the morning of 10 July 1944, and 46 Highland Brigade attacked eastwards towards Bretteville and Louvigny past this point. Further to the west, the Royal Engineers had prepared crossings for vehicles by clearing trees, grading the banks and by a certain amount of in-filling of the streambed. The 43rd Wessex's mortar platoons and forward divisional artillery batteries were positioned in the valley bottom. One gunner recalls that: *'The stream was clogged with corpses, ours and theirs, and was seen to run red with blood. This is where we got our "fresh" water from for several weeks.'*

FONTAINE ETOUPEFOUR AND LES DUANES

Drive on, following the D214 as it turns to the right and uphill from the valley bottom until a T-junction is reached by Fontaine Etoupefour Church. ➋**Turn right** and park up outside the church. This was an area of much activity on the morning of 10 July 1944. In the farms opposite the entrance to the church, were the tactical headquarters of both 130 and 214 Brigades, while the church tower offered the observer a view of most of the battlefield. The anchor OP of 112 Field Regiment RA was initially in the tower but moved forward onto the ridge once Chateau de Fontaine and Eterville were taken. From midday onwards, Major General Thomas used the tower as his OP and from this vantage-point, he gave his orders for the afternoon's attacks. From the church wall on the southern side of the graveyard, today's visitor can look down towards the modern roundabout and the estate of holiday homes. This area was used

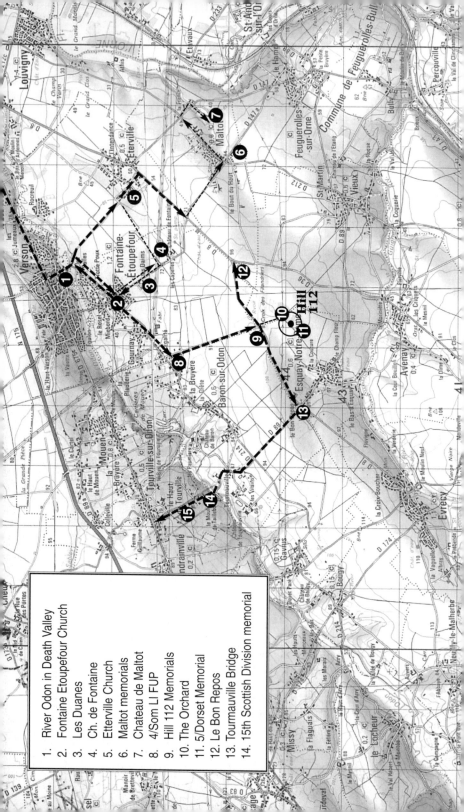

1. River Odon in Death Valley
2. Fontaine Etoupefour Church
3. Les Duanes
4. Ch. de Fontaine
5. Etterville Church
6. Maltot memorials
7. Chateau de Maltot
8. 4/Som LI FUP
9. Hill 112 Memorials
10. The Orchard
11. 5/Dorset Memorial
12. Le Bon Repos
13. Tourmauville Bridge
14. 15th Scottish Division memorial

by all three battalions of 130 Brigade as their forming up position. Return to your vehicle and head for the **roundabout**. Take the **third exit** and follow the **D147A** in the direction of Maltot. In passing, note the second turning from the roundabout into the new housing named *'Rue du General Breeden'* [sic]. Lieutenant Colonel Bredin commanded 5/Dorsets later in the war but in July 1944 he was second in command of 2/Dorsets in the Tilly sur Seulles area and did not take command of the 5/Dorsets until early 1945.

Continue up the road as it rises out of the valley. Almost as the last houses are passed the plane trees and honey coloured

❸ buildings of **les Duanes farm** complex comes into view. Here no man's land was very narrow. The farm was the initial objective of 5/Dorsets and was taken by C Company. The farm is private property but without trespassing, the visitor can appreciate the way that the soldiers of 2/22 SS Panzer Grenadiers would have fortified

Les Duanes farm.

the already strong buildings and surrounding paddocks. Easily visible from the church tower, the defenders of les Duanes were the victims of heavy and highly accurate artillery fire and 5/Dorsets were quickly among the stunned defenders.

CHATEAU de FONTAINE **❹**

Resume the journey to the south across open farmland that in 1944 was cloaked in waist-high wheat (modern varieties are much shorter). After **500 metres**, a brown tourist sign directs the visitor down a track **to the left**. This is the access to Chateau de Fontaine. Once on the track, look to the left. This is where 5/Dorsets 'Horseshoe' Wood, D Company's objective, used to be. The Comte du Lar opens the Chateau and his small museum of artefacts, mainly collected from his moat during dredging operations, at irregular intervals over the years. Visits to the chateau can be booked by phone. If you have booked a visit or the gate on the track down to the Chateau, between a double row of trees is open, **drive down** and park on the gravelled area. The Chateau was largely a

After the battle at Chateau de Fortaine and a group of visitors from 5/Dorsets. The Chateau and farm today. A large objective for a single company of Dorsets.

ruin in 1944 and marked as such on the 1:25,000 map. The battle further reduced the buildings. However, the present Count has restored the old gatehouse into a small house. The Chateau and the farm buildings to the west were at the centre of 2/22 Panzer Grenadier Regiment's defensive positions. Fighting through the Chateau and farm complex was a slow business for 5/Dorsets. It also took 7/Somerset LI, who replaced the captors, several days to winkle out the last snipers, some of whom, concealed in the moat and in the haystacks, caused many casualties. An obvious target for German *Nebelwerfers*, the area of the Chateau and farm received much attention and were dangerous places to linger in the open by night or day. A steady stream of casualties came back from here in the days following Operation JUPITER and added to the heavy toll of losses of 10 July 1944. Please do not wander around the farmyard. The visitor can see the main features of the farm from the area of the Chateau.

ETERVILLE ❺

Return to the end of the Chateau's drive. Here one can **park** and, **on foot, take the track** to **turn right** in an easterly direction towards Eterville. Be careful not to block the track with parked cars. Those not wishing to walk should return to the road and retrace the route back towards the Fontaine Etoupefour church on the **D 214** towards Caen and Odon Bridge. Just **before reaching the bridge**, take a turning to the **right**, up a narrow hedged road signposted to **Eterville (C1)**. Follow the road up out of the valley. 4/Dorsets advanced across the open ground to the right, from the area of the church. Note the convex shape of the ground, which meant that much of 4/Dorsets' advance was out of sight of 1/22 SS Panzer Grenadiers. The *Frundsberg's* outpost line lay along the crest and in the open fields just in front of the village edge.

Park by the **village sign**, at the ninety-degree bend to the left, where a track joins from the right. This is where those that walk the 800 metres from Chateau de Fontaine will emerge. The Germans had sited 75mm anti-tank guns in the hedgerow by this junction. Their field of fire to the front was short and would have meant engaging the thick frontal armour of attacking tanks. Consequently, the guns' main arcs of fire were to the left and right, where they could engage armoured vehicles approaching the village from the flanks, with a far greater probability of a kill. However, these guns, dug in without overhead cover, were destroyed by the bombardment. It is also in this area that Private Alfie Brown saw Germans running from the hedgerows as the Crocodile flame thrower tanks of 79th Armoured Division set the cover at the edge of the village on fire. By **walking** a short way along **the track** to the right, one can see the restored Eterville Chateau. Earlier in the campaign, this building had been a German hospital and in July 1944 still bore the red cross on its roof. At the time of the battle, it was in the frontline and with its associated farm buildings, made a formidable objective for the right hand companies of 4/Dorsets.

Return to your car and continue **along the forward edge of the village** towards the new buildings. The estate of modern houses has been built on what were, until the mid-nineties, orchards and paddocks. Follow the **tarmac road** around to the **right** and park by the short drive to the church. This was the location of 4/Dorsets' battalion headquarters. The avenue of trees is original but the flanking garden walls are much higher than they were in 1944. Sergeant Geoff Cleal dug his trench at the base of a tree halfway along on the left and the Commanding Officer's Bren gun carrier was parked immediately to the left of the double gates as one enters the churchyard. This is the scene of Corporal Chris Portway's game of cat and mouse, which ended with him throwing grenades into the church. Soon afterwards, it was to become the Regimental Aid Post (RAP) of 4/Dorsets. The church overflowed with British and German wounded and, consequently, those awaiting treatment or evacuation had to lie outside risking death or further wounds from shells and falling masonry. The extent of the church's rebuilding is readily apparent.

Return to your car but before getting in, take a moment to **walk a short way** down the track opposite, between the tall hedges. Here, one gets a good impression of what Eterville was like in 1944, when orchards, trees and hedges were more numerous, fields of fire shorter and most roads were, by modern standards, little more than tracks. **Return to your car**. The road was the centre line for the attack and boundary between 4/Dorsets' advancing companies. Battalion Headquarters was normally deployed somewhere near to the centre line just behind the advancing troops. In this case, Lieutenant Colonel Cowie found himself with his signallers in the frontline as the companies had diverged from the centre line towards the large farms in their sector.

Follow the **'Centre Line'** through the village. The Cameronians, who held the village against counter-attacks from I and II SS Panzer Corps, established their Battalion Headquarters at the slightly offset crossroads in the centre of the village. Continuing in a southerly direction, there is, on the left, a small road dedicated to the Dorsets. The road ahead was 4/Dorsets' objective. On reaching the junction, **turn right** on to the **D8 Caen to Evrecy** road. At the time of writing, a bypass is being built and foundations of new buildings are being laid. This will sadly destroy all traces of the ditch occupied by the Dorsets and Cameronians, as well as their field of fire.

MALTOT 6

After **three hundred metres**, turn **left** and take the **D147a** towards **Maltot**. You are now following the route taken by 7/Hampshires in their advance on the morning of 10 July 1944. They had advanced between Eterville and the water tower near the junction. The advance received little enemy attention until they had crossed the

The crossroads at the centre of Maltot then and now.

ridgeline and were moving down towards Maltot.

As one approaches Maltot, on the right of the road is la Ferme Neuve. This is far more extensive than it was, and the houses on the left extend further up the hill than they did in 1944. **Park on the verge** on the right, near the **track up to the farm**. From here, the visitor can see the western portion of Maltot and the ridges that dominate it. The ridge to the south-west made excellent fire positions for German tanks, who were 'jockeying' from position to position, thus avoiding destruction and giving the British the impression that they were heavily outnumbered. So great was the destruction in Maltot, little of the original village remains.

Drive on down to the **roundabout**. Here the villagers have erected a small black monument to their liberators. The stone commemorates the Dorsets but makes no mention of the Hampshires or indeed the Wiltshire battalions who finally captured and held the village on 23 July 1944! **Turn left** onto the **D 212** towards Caen. During Operation Express, 5/Wilts advanced on either side of that road. They fought through the ruins of the village 22 July, evening, 1944, driving the defenders from 272nd Infantry Division before them. The village was in the front line for almost a month and was almost totally destroyed. Most of the houses were rebuilt in the 1950s on original foundations but there has been some subsequent infilling.

At the end of the village, **drive on** through the open country for several hundred metres and take the **first turning** to the **right**. 4/Wilts fought in the broken country to your front and only made progress with difficulty. On the right is Chateau de Maltot. ❼ The massive stone walls survived the battle but it lay derelict for many years until the interior was replaced and the building taken into use as an agricultural college. The grand hall and staircase, where 4/Wilts and *Wehrmacht* Grenadiers exchanged bullets and grenades, are sadly no more. **Turn around** and **retrace** your steps back through

OXFAM

VAT: 348 4542 38

Volunteer here: Have fun,
meet new people & learn
new skills
Sign up in-store or at
www.oxfam.org.uk/jointheteam

COLIN	SALES	F7101/POS1

WEDNESDAY 7 JULY 2021   14:27 091164

| 1 | C10C - MILITARY | £2.99 |
| 1 | C10C - MILITARY | £2.99 |

GIFT AID 20123 1967 101

| 1 | C10E - OTHER HISTORY | £3.99 |

3 Items

TOTAL	**£9.97**
CREDIT CARD	£9.97

Oxfam Shop: F7101
1659 High Street
Knowle, B93 0LL
01564 773798
oxfam.org.uk/shop

Share your finds with
#FoundInOxfam

THANK YOU

Every item you buy or donate
helps beat poverty.

We offer a 30-day refund policy for items returned to store in the
condition they were sold in, with proof of purchase and with valid
price ticket attached to the item. View full T&Cs in-store or at
www.oxfam.org.uk/high-street-faqs

Our recycling centre saves 12,000
tonnes of clothing from going to
landfill every year

Maltot towards Fontaine Etoupefour.

At the **D 8 – D 147a** crossroads go **straight across**, passing Chateau Fontaine on the right and les Duanes on the left. At the FUP roundabout in Fontaine Etouperfour **turn left** on to the **D 214**, following the signpost **towards Baron**. The road west from the roundabout was the front line before the attack of 10 July 1944. To the left, the enemy were on Hill 112 and to the right in the bottom of the Odon Valley were the Wyverns' mortar platoons, positioned as far forward as possible to make the most of their 3,000 metre range. Just before the Baron commune signpost, **turn left** at the statue of the Virgin and Child, passing a few houses, orchard and paddocks. **Stop** as ❽ you emerge into open country. 4/Somerset LI advanced up Hill 112 astride this road. Note the concave slope that allowed the SS soldiers to observe every move on the low ground, which made 4/Somerset LI's capture of the line of the Caen to Evrecy road a considerable achievement. Continue up the road towards the Hill.

HILL 112

Where the modern Caen to Evrecy road crosses the ancient Roman Road, there is an obvious collection of memorials and flagpoles and a solar power generator. This is the plateau of Hill 112, although the spot height is actually by the pylon between the two woods four hundred metres to the south. The memorials, in various forms, have been placed at this point since 1945 to join older features that stood here during the battle. **Park** your car off the road alongside the new memorial. Beware of the cars that speed along the main road.

Other than the proliferation of monuments, the area is much the same as it was in July 1944, except that the poplars that lined the main road were not replanted after the war. The line of the road was 4/Somerset LI's first objective and it eventually became the British front line. Outposts were positioned along the low banks that edged the road, while the Battalion's main defences were dug in the fields to the north of the road, about thirty to forty metres down the hill.

THE ROMAN ROAD

The Romans first made the long straight and ancient way that bisects Hill 112 from north to south. Duke William used the part of the road that descends to the north during his 'shoes back to front' adventure and this portion is called *Chemin du Duc Guillaume*. This name is engraved on a small stone block by the road junction. This road was also the 'centre line' or axis of advance for 4/Som LI on the morning of 10 June 1944. The battalion was deployed in a box formation, with two companies on either side of the road. The unmade up but well defined extension to the south of the memorials was used at night by the infantry of both sides, as direction finding across shell marked country in the pitch black became increasingly difficult.

CROIX DES FILANDRIERS

The stone cross standing just to the south of the road pre-dates the battle by hundreds of years. It was erected to commemorate an improbable sounding incident when Duke William of Normandy, later our own King, William the Conqueror, was fighting his barons. The tale goes that as the Duke approached Hill 112 he took off his horse's shoes and replaced them backwards, in order deceive his pursuers into following the hoof prints in the wrong direction. The cross was originally known as *La Croix des fers en derrière* or literally translated as 'The shoes back to front'. The cross survived the battle with only a few minor strike marks from bullets and shrapnel on the German side. Veterans always marvel at the cross's durability, standing as it did on the front line, during a hell of steel and lead.

THE 43RD WESSEX DIVISION MEMORIAL

The first memorial to those who fell at Hill 112 was a simple sign erected by 5/DCLI in August 1944, once the breakout had taken the fighting south to Falaise. This sign bore the simple words 'Cornwall Wood'. Next came a large wooden monument erected by the French people from the surrounding area. Returning from the Army of Occupation in Germany during July 1945, the first visitors from the 43rd Wessex Division were greatly touched by the memorial raised by the local people in memory of those killed liberating them. The stone memorial raised by the 43rd Wessex replaced the wooden structure in the late 1940s. It is an irony that the memorial was carved by German masons in the town of Urelzen (near Belsen) on the North German Plain. The work was supervised by Bob Tingey of 260 Field Company Royal Engineers, who reported that 'the German masons were very reluctant and nervous about visiting France so soon after the end of the war'.

Memorials of a similar design stand at Wynyard's Gap in North Dorset and on Castle Hill at Mere in Wiltshire (only two minutes drive from the A303). A third memorial in England is set into the rock of Rough Tor in Cornwall. A Divisional Memorial Roll of Honour is on display at the Devonshire and Dorset Regiment Chapel in Exeter Cathedral.

THE HILL 112 FRENCH MONUMENT

Brainchild of the late mayor of Esquay, Antoine Lepeltier, the mound on which the memorial site was built in 1996. In its original form, it rose five metres above the surrounding area. However, without the opportunity to settle, the weight of the stone and concrete on top of the mound caused it to collapse. Rebuilt, the base of the memorial is now a wider but lower mound. The monument's central feature is the slate *table d'orientation*, bearing the shields of some of the regiments that fought at Hill 112. The three blanked out shields were SS badges that had to be removed, following protests, as the display of German emblems is illegal within Normandy. Surrounding the tableau and forming the boundary to the memorial are nineteen pillars, each engraved with the name of one of the surrounding villages and communes who contributed to the cost of the memorial project. Most of the pillars bear a cross and a number. This represents the number of civilians killed during the war, mostly in June and July 1944. The Caen pillar, for instance, records the figure 1970 of its citizens killed in its liberation. Nearer to Hill 112 the small village of Evrecy lost 132 of its people killed on 15 June 1944, in a bombing raid. Apparently the first wing of Allied aircraft came in, dropped its bombs and many people were buried in the ruins of their houses. Villagers from the surrounding area came in to dig them out but were caught in the second wave of bombing an hour or so later. Despite tragedies like this, the friendship and generosity of the local people to veterans who continue to visit Normandy has been remarkable.

MARK VII CHURCHILL TANK

Sergeant Albert Figg returned to Normandy with a party from the 43rd Wessex Association for the first time in 1998. He had been a Number One gunner on a 25-pounder of 477 Battery, 112/Field Regiment RA.

> *... we got used to certain grid references during Jupiter and the days afterwards and one occasion I remember saying, "Bloody hell! Firing on that hill again. Let's go up there and we will shift the bastards." Standing on that hill fifty years later with the infantry boys who were fighting there, I realized what it was like for them and the tankies and I was ashamed of my words all those years ago.*

Albert decided there and then that something more was needed by which to remember them. With remarkable zeal and energy a suitable tank was located in a bog on Thetford Army Training Area, recovered to a workshop and refurbished. The Vehicle Troop of the British Army's Royal Logistic Corps (with the help of a farm tractor!) moved the tank into position.

NORMANDIE TERRE-LIBÉRÉE (NTL) TOTEM

Eight routes around the Normandy battlefield have been established since 1994. They are well signposted and a blue totem marks each significant stop. The brief descriptions of the action printed on the totems are very basic but even so, not always 100 per cent correct. Leaflets showing the routes are readily available from all tourist offices. Hill 112 is on Route 4 - *L'Affrontement* (The Confrontation), which takes visitors around the British battles of late June and of July 1944.

THE ORCHARD AND THE SMALL WOOD ⑩ and ⑪

The track (the Roman Road) that leads towards the Orchard can be used to get a closer view of the much fought over area around the Hill 112 spot height. 5/DCLI attacked through 4/Som LI's positions on the slopes just below the road using this track as their axis of advance. The Small Orchard has now been removed. However, the Orchard remains much as it was when 5/DCLI and the SS Panzer Grenadiers fought for it, except that there are far fewer fruit trees within the hedge of tall trees. In fact, the Orchard is now used as a paddock which is normally home to Antoine Lepeltier's rather grumpy bull! Enter at your peril! Virtually all that there is to see is visible from the gate. Note the ditch that bisects the Orchard. This was the front line for most of 5/DCLI's stay on the feature. To the west of the track, under the pylon, there is a small memorial that reminds visitors in French, German and English to honour and respect those who fought on the Hill. Behind, there is a modern plantation that now fills the Paddock, which abuts the Small Wood, in which C Company 5/DCLI were lost virtually to a man. The trees was planted in commemoration of those who fell on Hill 112. **Walk on**, following the Roman Road to the south and **stop** at the **end of the hedge** on the right of the track. From here, one can appreciate what the battle was all about. Possession of the spectacular views across the countryside to the south would have given the British Artillery observers a significant advantage and is what the II SS Panzer Corps fought so hard to deny to the British. **Return to your car**.

5/Dorsets' Memorial ⑫

In order to visit 5/Dorsets' memorial, head towards Caen for half a mile. The memorial, on your right, stands in the apex of the first road junction. Park on the verge, off the road. The Battalion chose to set up its memorial at this spot (in the area of 4/Wiltshires' JUPITER objective), as it overlooks both Chateau de Fontaine and Maltot and is near to the site of the Triangular Wood. This wood, in fact a hedged orchard, was just to the south of the junction but sadly, it has been removed. Return to your car. Drive past the 43rd Wessex Division monument on the left and head in a westerly direction towards le Bon Repos crossroads.

LE BON REPOS ⑬

Park by the Elf garage. This is possibly one of the most inaptly named spots on the entire battlefield, literally meaning 'The Good Rest'. In the frontline for almost a month, those soldiers of both sides who fought at le Bon Repos got precious little sleep. During Operation JUPITER, 5/Wilts attacking over the ridge to the north of the road and on an exposed slope immediately got into trouble. On 23 July 1944, the road from Hill 112 to le Bon Repos was used as the axis of advance for the raid by 4/Welch, 107/Regt RAC and the Crocodiles of 141/Regiment RAC. The expanding village of Esquay has crept up the hill towards le Bon Repos since the war. In 1944 the crossroads hamlet was a separate community. **Turn right** at the crossroads. 2/Glasgow Highlanders attacked down this slope to capture the hamlet on the night of 15/16 July 1944. Imagine the terrible sight of the Crocodiles' lances of flame burning out the defenders in the buildings. Follow the road on, over the crest, following signs to Tourville.

⑭

TOURMAUVILLE BRIDGE

After following the bends down into the Odon Valley, the visitor reaches the Tourmauville bridge seized by 2/Argyles on 27 June, completing the first phase of Operation Epsom. **Park** in the small lay-by on the left just before the bridge. Beware of the traffic. The NTL totem describes the action.

⑮

15TH SCOTTISH DIVISION MEMORIAL

Follow the road out of the valley. On the left is the memorial to the 15th Scottish Division. It stands on the hillside overlooking the high watermark of the Division's first battle of the campaign. It is an unusual memorial, in that it records the divisional order of battle, including the often neglected divisional troops. This is the last stop on the tour.

Drive on to the **T-junction** in Tourville. Depending on your eventual destination, turn left for Villers Bocage and Bayeux or right to Caen.

THE CEMETERIES

Many visitors to the Normandy battlefields do not feel that their tour is complete without having paid their respects to the dead at a military cemetery. However, there are no cemeteries in the area covered by this book but details of three British and one German cemeteries linked to the battles are given below.

Initially, most of those killed in action in the Hill 112 area were buried on the battlefield near the spot where they fell. Others, who died of wounds while they were being evacuated, were interred at cemeteries that formed alongside medical units. There were also several hundred soldiers of the Wessex Division listed as 'Missing' after the battle and a high proportion of these have no known grave. Following the experience of the First World War, it was decided that graves in battlefield cemeteries would be concentrated into a few larger post-war cemeteries. Most of the dead from Hill 112 are to be found in three of the eighteen Commonwealth War Graves Commission (CWGC) Cemeteries in Normandy.

There are several options available for visitors to find and visit individual graves. The easiest is through the Commonwealth War Graves Commission Head Office, whose address is at the end of this chapter. Those with access to the Internet, can visit the CWGC web site at http:/yard.ccta.gov.uk/cwgc. The web site can be a great help in finding Hill 112 casualties as it has, amongst other features, a date based search capability. This combined with use of the Order of Battle, see page 189, will enable the visitor to make a list of JUPITER graves to visit. Regimental Headquarters and military museums are good sources of information and advice but, unless the visitor lives near by and is prepared to personally look things up, it is recommended, that you avoid sending queries to them. Regimental Headquarters, have over the years, been heavily cut and are, consequently, understaffed. They normally have to request a donation of £10 - £15 for their services. Copies of CWGC registers, detailing all graves in individual cemeteries are, however, to be found in the metal-fronted register box at each cemetery.

Banneville-la-Campagne CWGC Cemetery.

This cemetery contains the remains of many soldiers who died in areas of the battlefield that remained as either No Man's Land or were held by the Germans on or shortly after 10 July 1944. When Maltot and Hill 112 were taken in late July and early August 1944 respectively, many bodies were not fit for immediate recovery and were buried as nearby. Sergeant Geoff Cleal was the 4/Dorsets' Battalion Orderly Room Sergeant and the sight, after two weeks of lying unburied in the sun, of the blackened, rotting corpses of his comrades was shocking. His unenviable task was to identify the bodies from his battalions of 'missing'. Few men who entered the stinking ruins of Maltot will ever forget the experience.

Banneville-la-Campagne lies eight kilometres to the east of Caen on the N174 and should not be confused with the Canadian cemetery with a similar name further south towards Falaise. From the centre of Caen find the station (Gare SNCF) and follow the *Autres Directions* to the *Périphérique*. Turn onto the N175 and head towards Liseux and Sannerville. The cemetery is on the right-hand side, about a kilometre from the village of Sannerville. It is recommended that the visitor avoids the A13 / E46 as an unnecessary toll is payable on exit and matters are complicated by the Sannerville/Troan junction having only entry and exits to and from the eastbound carriageway.

The cemetery lies one hundred metres south of the N175. Access is via a beautiful curving and well-maintained grass path, lined with shrubs. For the most part the cemetery contains graves dating from the Normandy campaign's Jupiter period up to the closure of the Falaise gap at the end of August 1944. There are now 2,175 Allied graves in the Banneville Cemetery alone. The founding principles, design and layout are of the style typical of most CWGC cemeteries established since the Great War. The overall look and feel is one of a quiet English garden. The main features of Banneville (and most other CWGC cemeteries) are the Cross of Sacrifice and the altar-like Stone of Remembrance, built in Portland stone, with the inscription 'THEIR NAME LIVETH FOR EVERMORE'. The gravestones, also of the same white stone, are surrounded by plants from the British Isles. One of the most touching features of the British War Cemeteries is the principle of equality of treatment. Officers lie alongside ordinary soldiers with exactly the same style of gravestone.

Some details of a few of the graves from the fighting on Hill 112 are listed below.

The Commanding Officer of 5/DCLI, Lieutenant Colonel Dick James lies in Plot X, Row G, grave 15. He was shot out of a tree on the morning of 11 July 1944 while directing the artillery fire that was so important in maintaining his battalion's position on Hill 112. The visitor will notice that the regimental badge on his gravestone is that of the Somerset Light Infantry. This is not a mistake. Officers and those serving with other units, such as commandos, have the badge of their parent regiment, which is not necessarily the one with which they were serving when they were killed. In this case, Dick James had been commissioned in the Somerset Light Infantry and had only taken command of 5/DCLI a few days before his death in action on Hill 112.

Saint Manvieu CWGC Cemetery, Cheux

Of the graves dating from 10 July 1944 in this cemetery, most were killed in the frontline or on spots that were taken during JUPITER. During the battle covered by this book, forward dressing stations were established along the Caen to Villers Bocage road, with one of the brigade's field ambulance units being based at Chateau Mouen. The more seriously wounded were passed back to units where life saving surgery could be performed. These were in the area of Cheux. In Saint Manvieu, there are 2,183 graves dating from the period between mid-June and mid -July 1944. Included are four plots totalling 556 German graves, many of whom would have been prisoners who died of wounds while in Allied care. Given that the majority of the German formations fighting to the west of Caen were from I and II SS Panzer Corps, it is reasonable to conclude that many were SS soldiers. The usual practice of converting *Waffen* SS ranks to their *Wehrmacht* equivalent has been followed here.

Quite a few of the graves in St Manvieu belong to the Royal Tank Regiment. That of Second Lieutenant George Hendrie, commander of 1 Troop A Squadron 9/RTR, is to be found in plot VIII, row E, grave 13. He was killed by an armour-piercing shot that just missed his tank *Impudent*'s turret but decapitated him as he advanced towards Maltot in support of 7/Hampshires.

Another casualty of the fighting in 130 Brigade's area was Captain Paul Cash of 112 (Wessex) Field Regiment RA, aged twenty-six years. He was the fourth Forward Observation Officer of 220 Battery to be killed. He died of wounds on 13 July 1944, when a shell exploded above his trench in the area of Chateau de Fontaine. He had been slightly wounded in the face during the first day of JUPITER. He was awarded a Military Cross for coolly and accurately supporting 7/Hampshire and 4/Dorsets in Maltot. He left a son named William, whom he never met. This son is now a senior backbench Westminster MP.

Lieutenant Colonel WD Blacker DSO, another gunner, also lies at rest at Saint Manvieu. He was killed at Chateau de Fontaine on 11 July 1944 when a *Nebelwerfer* bomb landed in the back of his White half-track OP and Tactical CP vehicle. The lightly armoured sides of the vehicle gave protection against shell splinters and small arms fire but its canvas roof offered no protection at all. Colonel Blacker was the third commanding officer in the Wessex Division to be killed during Operation JUPITER

Bayeux War Cemetery and Memorial

Located on the Bayeux ring road (originally created by the Royal Engineers to avoid the city's narrow streets) to the south of the city are Normandy's main British cemetery and the memorial to the missing. Both were designed by the noted CWGC architect, Phillip Hepworth. The dead (4,648) who lie in the cemetery come from actions fought all over Normandy and are largely but not exclusively, those who died of wounds. The area to the south-west of the city was where the majority of the field hospitals were located in the Second Army's Rear Maintenance Area. Serious casualties were tended until they were stabilized and fit to be flown or taken by ship to the UK. Sadly, however, a significant proportion died. The majority of the graves (3,935) are British. However, no less than ten other nationalities are represented among the dead, including four hundred and sixty-six Germans, who were mainly wounded prisoners of war. There is only one soldier listed as Unknown. This is a reflection of the fact that most soldiers who lie in Bayeux died of wounds and were not moved here from battlefield cemeteries, where wounds and time frequently removed traces of individuals' identity.

Across the road is the memorial to those who are missing and consequently have no known grave. It lists 1,805 names of Commonwealth soldiers who lost their lives between the D-Day assault on the Normandy beaches and the crossing of the Seine. The Latin inscription is translated as 'We, once conquered by William, have now set free the Conqueror's native land'

German War Cemetery Saint Desir-de-Lisieux

This is one of six German War Graves Welfare Organization cemeteries in the invasion area of Normandy. It is four kilometres west of Lisieux on the N13. Buried here are 3,735 soldiers, making this by far the smallest German cemetery in Normandy. As with the British dead from the fighting at Hill 112, the bodies have ended up scattered across the various cemeteries but a high proportion of those at Saint Desir date from the 10 July period. The contrast between Commonwealth War Graves Commission cemeteries and those of the Germans is marked. The mass nature of the burials and the representative style of grave marking, beside the differences in style and layout, are the most obvious variations.

Order of Battle HILL 112
43 WESSEX DIVISION

HQ 43rd (WESSEX) INFANTRY DIVISION
43rd (Wessex) Divisional Signals Regiment (-)

HQ 129th INFANTRY BRIGADE
4th Battalion, The Somerset Light Infantry
4th Battalion, The Wiltshire Regiment
5th Battalion, The Wiltshire Regiment
94th (Dorset and Hampshire) Field Regiment RA
235th Anti-Tank Battery
206th Field Company Royal Engineers
A (Machinegun) Company 8th Middlesex (including
a Heavy Mortar Platoon)
129th Field Ambulance
Support Troop 360th Light Anti-Aircraft Battery
30th Independent Anti-Aircraft Troop
2nd Company Divisional Signal Regiment
504th Company Royal Army Service Corps

HQ 130th INFANTRY BRIGADE
7th Battalion, The Hampshire Regiment
4th Battalion, The Dorsetshire Regiment
5th Battalion, The Dorsetshire Regiment
112th (Wessex) Field Regiment Royal Artillery
233rd Anti-Tank Battery
553rd Field Company Royal Engineers
B (Machinegun) Company 8th Middlesex (including
a Heavy Mortar Platoon)
130th Field Ambulance
Support Troop 362nd Light Anti-Aircraft Battery
32nd Independent Anti-Aircraft Troop
3rd Company 43rd Divisional Signals Regiment
505th Company Royal Army Service Corps

HQ 214th INFANTRY BRIGADE
7th Battalion Somerset Light Infantry
1st Battalion The Worcestershire Regiment
5th Battalion Duke of Cornwall's Light Infantry
179th Field Regiment Royal Artillery
333rd Anti-Tank Battery Royal Artillery
204th Field Company Royal Engineers
C (Machinegun) Company 8th Middlesex (including
a Heavy Mortar Platoon)
213th Field Ambulance
Support Troop 361st Light Anti-Aircraft Battery
31st Independent Anti-Aircraft Troop
4th Company 43rd Divisional Signal Regiment
54th Company Royal Army Service Corps

43rd WESSEX DIVISIONAL TROOPS
43rd Recconnisance Regiment (Not in action)
HQ 59th Anti-Tank Regiment Royal Artillery
(Gloucesters) and 236th Battery
HQ 110th Light Anti-Aircraft Regiment RA (7th
Dorsets), 360th Battery (-), 361st Battery (-) and
362nd Battery (-)
HQ 43rd Division Engineers Regiment, 207th Field
Park Company and 43rd Divisional Postal Unit
HQ 8th (Machinegun) Battalion, The Middlesex Regt
Royal Army Service Corps HQ 43rd Division RASC
Battalion and 506th Company RASC
Royal Army Medical Corps   14th Field Dressing
Section, 15th Field Dressing Section and 38th Field
Hygiene Section
Royal Army Ordnance Corps 43rd Division Ordnance
Field Park and 306th Mobile Bath Unit
Royal Electrical and Mechanical Engineers 129th
Infantry Brigade Workshop, 130th Infantry Brigade
Workshop and 214th Infantry Brigade Workshop
Military Police 43rd Division Company Royal Corps
of Military Police
Intelligence Corps 57th Field Security Section

4th ARMOURED BRIGADE
The Royal Scots Greys
3rd County of London Yeomanry (The
Sharpshooters)
44th Royal Tank Regiment
2nd Battalion, King's Royal Rifle Corps
4th Regiment Royal Horse Artillery
144th (Self Propelled) Anti-Tank Battery RA
4th Armoured Brigade Signal Squadron

31st TANK BRIGADE
7th Royal Tank Regiment
9th Royal Tank Regiment
31st Armoured Brigade Signal Squadron

XII CORPS TROOPS
86th Anti-Tank Regiment RA (5th Prince of Wales's)
128th Battery, 129th Battery (M10), 130th Battery
and 340th Battery (M10)

21st ARMY GROUP TROOPS
3rd Army Groups Royal Artillery
8th Army Groups Royal Artillery
79th ARMOURED DIVISION TROOPS
          141st Regiment RAC (Crocodiles)

SS Ranks and their British and US equivalents

Waffen SS		British Army	US Army
SS-*Brigadeführer*		Brigadier	Brigadier General
SS-*Oberführer*		(not applicable)	Senior Colonel
SS-*Standartenführer*		Colonel	Colonel
SS-*Obersturmbannführer*		Lieutenant Colonel	Lieutenant Colonel
SS-*Sturmbannführer*		Major	Major
SS-*Hauptsturmführer*		Captain	Captain
SS-*Obersturmführer*		Lieutenant	1st Lieutenant
SS-*Untersturmführer*		2nd Lieutenant	2nd Lieutenant
SS-*Sturmscharführer*		Regimental Sergeant Major	Sergeant Major
SS-*Hauptscharführer*		Sergeant Major	Master Sergeant
SS-*Oberscharführer*		(not applicable)	Technical Sergeant
SS-*Scharführer*		Colour Sergeant	Staff Sergeant
SS-*Unterscharführer*		Sergeant	Sergeant
SS-*Rottenführer*		Corporal	Corporal
SS-*Sturmmann*		Lance Corporal	(not applicable)
SS-*Oberschütze*		(not applicable)	Private 1st Class
SS-*Mann*		Private	Private